Out of the Fog

Breaking Up with Alcohol
and Living a Life of Passion and Purpose

Jenn Burton

Leaning Rock Press
Gales Ferry, CT 06335

Leaning Rock Press
Gales Ferry, CT 06335
leaningrockpress@gmail.com
www.leaningrockpress.com

Copyeditor: Florence Kilgo

978-1-960596-34-5, Hardcover
978-1-960596-35-2, Softcover

Library of Congress Control Number: 2024913136

Publisher's Cataloging-in-Publication Data
(Prepared by Cassidy Cataloguing's PCIP Service)

Names:	Burton, Jenn, author.
Title:	Out of the fog : breaking up with alcohol and living a life of passion and purpose / Jenn Burton.
Description:	Gales Ferry, CT : Leaning Rock Press, [2024]	Includes bibliographical references.
Identifiers:	ISBN: 978-1-960596-34-5 (hardcover)	978-1-960596-35-2 (softcover)	LCCN:2024913136
Subjects:	LCSH: Burton, Jenn.	Recovering alcoholics--Biography.	Women alcoholics--Biography	Alcoholism--Psychological aspects.	Alcoholism--Social aspects.	Women--Mental health.	Self-actualization (Psychology) in women.	LCGFT: Autobiographies.	BISAC: SELF-HELP / Substance Abuse & Addictions / Alcohol.
Classification:	LCC: HV5137 .B87 2024	DDC: 362.292082--dc23

Printed in the United States of America

Dedication

To my husband and four beautiful children.
You will forever be my why.

Table of Contents

Chapter 1

Good-Girl Training Grounds

I haven't had a drink in eight days. I know that might not seem like much to many of you, but it's been a different kind of eight days than during previous attempts to stop drinking. However, before we get into all of that, let's start at the beginning. I'm what you might call a typical child of the 1980s, conditioned to be a good girl, not make too much noise, and try to fit in with my peers. The messaging directed at us didn't come from TikTok or Instagram, but we still heard and saw those messages loud and clear from magazines, TV shows, movies, and music.

According to Glennon Doyle in her memoir, *Untamed,* "Ten is when we learn how to be good girls and real boys. Ten is when children begin to hide who they are in order to become what the world expects them to be. Right around ten is when we begin to internalize our formal taming. Ten is when the world sat me down, told me to be quiet, and pointed toward my cages…"[1] Until I read this, I thought I was just one of the unlucky ones who grew up plagued by depression and anxiety, always working extra hard to make the people around me happy and killing myself to fit into this box that society had created for me.

---

[1]   Doyle, Glennon. *Untamed,* The Dial Press, 2020, 4.

It has taken a lot of self-reflection and internal emotional work to recognize that I am a product of the good-girl generation and that I grew up tamed. This comment is by no means a knock on my childhood or the way I was raised, because, if you could handpick parents, you'd pick mine without a doubt. My upbringing is a reflection of the larger culture, societal norms, and gender stereotypes—and most of us can probably assert a similar thing. The expectation for girls to grow up "good" and "tamed" was hardwired into my peers and me from the earliest age. Girls who grew up in the late 1990s were taught to be quiet, obedient, and small. I understood the assignment, and, a shy kid, I also felt things more deeply than my sister or my peers. I recognized from a young age that I felt things differently than others around me. I'm also learning about HSPs (highly sensitive persons) and have found that there's a high likelihood that I am an HSP. If I am, it explains so much about how I always felt more emotional, more of a crybaby, more sensitive than other kids my age. I see some of those traits in two of my children, and I think there's a strong chance that one of my parents is an HSP too. Some of us are more affected by our surroundings than others, and while that can feel heavy at times, it's a beautiful thing too. As Elaine Aron writes, "We are a package deal, however. Our trait of sensitivity means we will also be cautious, inward, needing extra time alone. Because people without the trait (the majority) do not understand that, they see us as timid, shy, weak, or that greatest sin of all, unsociable. Fearing these labels, we try to be like others. But that leads to our becoming . . . distressed."[2]

The biggest issues I have had with making choices for myself is that I am always more concerned with how my decisions will affect the people around me. Parents, siblings, significant others, friends, children. Their needs and wants come before mine, because I am a people pleaser, an HSP, an empath, and a good girl at my core. That's what I was taught and trained to be, not because my parents wanted

---

2   Aron. Elaine, *The Highly Sensitive Person*, Kensington Publishing Corp., 1996, 5.

that for me, or because I chose it for myself, but because that is what culture and the media and my peers all showed me I should be. Instead of rebelling against those expectations, I have often made sacrifices in order to make the lives of others around me easier.

I have sacrificed a lot over the years. A single mom when my twins were babies, I sacrificed pursuing a teaching career at the college level. Then, I needed a stable profession that allowed for some flexibility, when I was a single mom to my twins, who had become toddlers. I continued to work in a career that I don't love because it afforded me flexibility as a mom and provided stability. I was offered a teaching position as adjunct faculty at my alma mater in 2012, but was refused the opportunity to take the position when my full-time job in human resources didn't allow me to adjust my hours to accommodate teaching one evening class a week. A dream was suddenly shattered, hopes were dashed, and my spirits crushed. But I knew I needed that full-time income to support my kids and be a wage-earning partner to my new husband. I sacrificed what I wanted for the good of those around me. I learned to quietly suffer from a very early age. I internalized my suffering so that I didn't inconvenience anyone else. I was a good girl and suppressed all of my disappointment because my needs and wants didn't matter as much. I believed all the hype about sacrificing your own wants and needs if you wanted to have a partnership and be a good parent.

I'm sure many of you have made sacrifices over the years that made you a good girl or a good parent or a sacrificial lamb in one way or another. But the narrative is changing. Therapists across the country recognize the "good-girl syndrome" that was hardwired into so many of us, especially in my generation, because our parents worked extra hard to make us happy since they didn't have the best childhoods. To prevent their own children from enduring similar upbringings, they did everything in their power to make sure we never wanted for anything or had to suffer in any way. Now, I see parents of my generation bending over backwards and paying thousands of dollars a month for travel sports, or dance, or whatever their kids are into, because they hope that buys them happiness and prevents them from suffering or dealing with hard things.

Studies involving generational gaps and stereotypes have always been interesting to me. I think our cultural beliefs and our historical circumstances can definitely have an impact on how we view the world. As an American Studies major in college, I was always drawn to the study of adolescence as a quintessential American ideal, something that doesn't really exist in other cultures across the world. I was drawn to the study of women in American society, and how religion and ethnicity shape our worldview. Becoming a parent in my twenties, I was suddenly entrusted with raising two human beings (not just one, but two at the same time!) and that taught me just how much I didn't know about the world. Who in their right mind decided to just hand the keys over to raising the next generation to those who arguably still hadn't figured out how to be adults at the turn of the twenty-first century? My graduating class was a cohort of cuspy millennials who experienced Y2K during their senior year of high school. We turned eighteen during a time when some people were doomsday prepping and really thought the world was ending at the strike of midnight on January 1, 2000. The type of upbringing we experienced varied from being latchkey kids to having overly protective parents who had survived unspeakable things during their own childhoods and did their best to prevent their own kids from feeling any pain. We didn't talk about money or finances. We just expected to live a cozy life, as long as we did what we were told. Society told us girls that we could go to college and have dreams. But we should also make sure to consider how that played into our future family life as the default parent while our husbands were out earning the big bucks. We were told that we could dream, but not too big. We could have goals, but nothing too "out there." We had to stay within the box that society had built for us, make good choices, and stay mostly tamed so we could find a man who wanted to marry us despite our audacity to have objectives and dreams of our own. The messaging may have been less loud and in your face than it was in the 1950s, but, I assure you, most of us, young women coming of age at the turn of the twenty-first century, heard it loud and clear.

I grew up in Southern California in a nice house, and my dad worked full-time while my mom worked a schedule that allowed her to be home with us in the afternoon, so we were never in daycare. When we were really young, my grandma, my dad's mom, watched my sister and me on occasion. My grandma was and still is one of my favorite humans on the planet. Regardless of what stupid life choices I've made along the way, she's always been my biggest fan and cheered me on from the sidelines. When others in my family were less than thrilled with my decision to move out at age eighteen, my grandma would come visit me at my apartment and take me to lunch. She's always shown me kindness, support, and love and I'm so grateful that I've gotten to have her in my life for the last forty-two years. She is pure gold, and I will always treasure our time together.

I was the younger daughter of a four-person household until I was about seven years old. My older sister and I are two and a half years apart. When I was seven, my parents started doing foster care and later adopted a baby boy. By the time I was nine years old, I had two younger brothers and was now a middle child. As far back as I can remember, I was a perfectionist and a good girl. I wanted everything that I did to be perfect and without flaws. I idolized my older sister. I wanted to make sure I didn't do anything to draw unwanted attention to myself, so I mostly stayed quiet and did what was expected of me at home and at school.

A pretty good kid, quiet and sensitive, and a big reader, I also loved playing soccer. I started playing when I was about six years old. I played on a competitive team and on my high school teams until I was eighteen years old. I played for fun in adult leagues off and on after that, but it was truly one of the solid pillars of my childhood and teenage years. It kept me in shape, it kept me aware of the necessity of working as a team, a skill I'd later need in jobs and in marriage and parenting for sure! My dad was my soccer coach for most of those years, aside from the high school teams I played on. He wasn't the kind of coach that took it easy on his kids, which I appreciate more than words can say. The fact that I was treated like everyone else gave me a strong work ethic. It taught me that I needed to put effort into everything I wanted (a starting forward position on the high school soccer team, for one), that life doesn't give us handouts, and we should be proud of the work we do to achieve our objectives.

I also had an incredibly tough, in-your-face best friend named Natalie since I was a very young girl. Her cousins lived on the same street as I, and she spent a lot of time in our neighborhood. I was an emotional kid, and she was always there to protect me from the kindergarten bullies. She's someone I still value very much to this day—someone who has been there for me through thick and thin, no matter how crazy each of our journeys has been. She's incredible and I look up to her strength, her grit, and her "I can do whatever I want" attitude. Natalie didn't have an easy life. She had a tough childhood, with parents who were in active addiction, and she herself struggled with addiction for many years. We drifted apart as kids, but always found our way back to each other. She's one of the people I admire most in this world. She has been sober for eighteen years and is a go-getter, with two small businesses, three kids, and a house with a white picket fence. She's an inspiration. And she always stood up for me, until I found my own voice and learned how to stick up for myself. One of my favorite photos of us, which my mom has somewhere in her photo collection, was taken on Halloween when we were probably six or seven years old and we both dressed up as Wonder Woman. She is truly a wonderful, superhero of a woman and I absolutely adore her. I've also learned a lot from her over the years, about myself and how the world works.

Soccer was life for many years. It was my weekend activity, practices twice a week (or more), and a commitment to be the best version of myself. At home, for hours, I would practice my juggling and ball-control skills. I analyzed plays in games where I could have done something better. I built strong bonds with my teammates, and some of them became my best friends for years to come. I firmly believe that youth sports (and any type of activity for young kids that requires them to be part of a team and do their part for the better of the unit as a whole) are a great tool to equip future generations with a sense of what real life can be like. And sports give them an opportunity to flex their "work it out" mental muscles when things get tough in life.

I found purpose in soccer. I found passion. Those are two things I feel like I've been searching for in my life since I became an adult. I found it once again in my college academic career, and then again in parenting. Now, as my kids are getting to the point where they don't necessarily need me every waking moment for their survival, I am feeling the crunch yet again to find that THING that makes me feel like I am living a life full of passion and purpose. Call it a midlife crisis. Call it a midlife unraveling (thanks to Brené Brown for that judicious description!). Whatever you call it, I'm having it. I turned forty in 2022, two years after a global pandemic that made me a full-time homeschooling mom of a kindergartener and first grader, plus a parent needing to manage two middle schoolers at home full-time. We were a house of chaos before, but COVID really threw me for a loop. I'd worked remotely for six years prior to COVID. I had a routine with the kids in school or of toddler ages, where I could distract them for chunks at a time, and baby and toddler noises in the background of a phone call (we didn't do much video calling in my early days of remote working) weren't that obnoxious. When you have four kids chasing each other through the house with kitchen utensils or plastic light sabers, because they're all losing their minds being cooped up together twenty-four seven, that's a whole different ball game. I definitely hit a point during the pandemic where drinking and numbing out became my survival mechanism. It's what got me from one day to the next, because I had something to look forward to, my "me time" in the evenings, when everything was a little calmer or at least I could pretend it was.

In her 2023 book, Celeste Yvonne discusses mommy wine culture and the plethora of wine memes circulating online during the global pandemic caused by COVID-19 in 2020. Yvonne writes, "Where some might have seen just a funny wine meme, I saw justification to drink. Where some might have seen a brief, breezy read about the benefits of wine, I found validation for what was becoming an increasingly troubling habit for me."[3] For many of us, pandemic parenting was not something we signed up for. Sure, we signed up to have the kids, but we didn't ever anticipate a global pandemic literally keeping us locked up together twenty-four seven for weeks and months on end. It was a scary time for a lot of people. Suddenly, moms were feeling even more isolated than ever, as the mental load that already overwhelms many of us was suddenly multiplied by the unknowns of the pandemic, non-stop parenting while still working from home in many cases, and juggling the emotions of kids who didn't understand what was going on in the world either. It. Was. A. Lot.

In response to this extra heavy weight added to our already crippling mental load, moms united in this understanding that wine would make it all better, and that every other mom was doing it too, so it was OK. Wine o'clock came earlier and earlier during the pandemic, to the point that one in three adults was drinking from home while working. According to an April 2020 article by the American Addiction Centers, "Chief Medical Officer Dr. Lawrence Weinstein was interviewed in Healthline speaking about an Alcohol.org study that determined about 1 in 3 Americans are drinking alcohol while working from home during the pandemic."[4] While advertising and memes on social media told us that drinking was more than normal because we were all stuck at home, studies continued to show the negative effects on mental health caused by drinking to excess during the pandemic.

---

3   Yvonne, Celeste, *It's Not About the Wine: The Loaded Truth behind Mommy Wine Culture*, Broadleaf Books, 2023, 97.

4   https://americanaddictioncenters.org/media/more-people-are-drinking-while-working-from-home-during-covid-19

My need to rely on crutches of all kinds to help me deal with emotions I had to suppress did not just arise when I was an adult. The passion-filled life that soccer brought to me as a kid and a teenager ended abruptly. I had a serious ankle injury my freshman year of high school at age fourteen. I was told in the emergency room that it was a sprain. But it turns out, after months of pain and not recovering, that I actually had suffered a hairline fracture that never fully healed. The result was that a piece of my ankle bone chipped off and floated around in my ankle, causing tons of issues. After several months, the injury had not healed and I ended up having surgery. Meanwhile, I had been cleared to play soccer after about six weeks from the initial injury so I had been out on the field playing with a broken ankle taped up, to the point I couldn't feel anything for a few months. That surgery resulted in my being sidelined for another several months as I went through physical therapy and the healing process. I gained weight, I found comfort in food, and I was continuing to engage in self-injury on a very regular basis. My mental health was not OK, because my passion and my purpose in life had been removed. It was an ugly time in my life, and one that my parents were not entirely equipped to deal with. We're talking about the late 1990s here (or the 1900s, as my ten-year-old would say in horror).

Mental health, depression, and anxiety were not things that we talked about on a regular basis in the 1990s and early 2000s. Those were things you dealt with in your home quietly and didn't share with the rest of the world. So, we all dealt with it in our own ways, as best as we knew how at the time. I was miserable. I planned out how many days a week I could stay home from school "sick" because I simply didn't want to be around other human beings. My parents did everything they could to support me, to try to make me happy during that time, but it was just awful all around. I had learned that if I wanted to fly under the radar and not cause waves, I needed to control the pain I was feeling emotionally. I would suffer in silence, and found ways to make my emotional pain something that I could control until I discovered self-injury. It started out before I was thirteen years old, with simple things. Banging my hand extra hard on the brick wall when we were playing outside in our backyard, or scraping the end of a paper clip across the back of my hand a little too hard. It developed into a full-on addiction to self-injury sometime around my thirteenth birthday, and continued into my adult years. Like my unhealthy relationship with alcohol in later years, my addiction to self-injury was something I battled quietly for more years of my life than not.

Thankfully, after months of physical therapy, I was able to get my ankle strong again so that I could play soccer. I was fully committed to getting into shape and back onto the field in my regular spot on the team. At the same time, I had started talking more frequently to an old friend from middle school who was trying to convince me to switch to a private Christian school she'd started attending her sophomore year. It was toward the end of my sophomore year by the time I was able to start walking normally again, and, over that summer, my parents and I decided that a change of scenery and the support of this old friend would be good for me. Having grown up in a Christian household and having attended a Christian school from fifth to eighth grade, I thought this might be a good change of pace for me. I'd alienated most of the friends I had at my current high school over the course of my sophomore year, and it's also where my older sister was a social butterfly, so I decided a new school where no one knew I was her little sister would be a nice fresh start.

The summer before my junior year was spent working out, getting back into soccer shape, losing the fiftyish pounds I had gained and getting back to my slim one-hundred-and-fifteen-pound soccer figure. I'd lost myself so much that year and I was focused on getting back onto the soccer field for the new season in August. It didn't hurt that I'd be starting at my new school in a body that I felt more comfortable in also. I still wore baggy clothes because I'd gotten used to that over the course of my sophomore year. Photos of me at the beginning of my junior year to the end show that I got much more comfortable in my own skin that year, for many different reasons.

But I felt during that summer that I was coming back to myself, and I was forming a really tight friendship with my friend Sarah. She was instrumental to my survival during that time. We had sleepovers at each other's houses every weekend, practically. She helped me find a confidence that I hadn't had in a really long time, and I will forever be grateful to her for the friend she was during those formative years, and the friend she remained throughout some of the hardest years of my young adult life down the road. She's a gem of a human being, and I'm lucky that I get to be her friend.

Junior year, I was starting at a new school. I was back on the soccer field in my rightful place as left forward with girls I'd been playing with (and winning championships with) for years. I was finally feeling like I had found my purpose again. And then I met him. The boy that I didn't know then would teach me so many things over the course of the next twenty-plus years. He's still teaching me things to be honest, but now the lessons are basically what not to do unless you want to screw up your relationship with people forever.

Funny how junior year of high school was the year I met this boy and also the year I had my first sip of alcohol. It's interesting how at the same time we start to become who we are, we grasp at anything that makes us feel something. For me, feelings of wanting to be loved and needing to fill up an empty space inside, that just couldn't be filled no matter how much of something I tried to take in—whether it was admiration from boys, or alcohol, or self-inflicted pain—was an unending pursuit. The more I tried to fill these bottomless needs the more the needs grew. So, I kept trying . . . to fill up the empty space, to feel something, to be needed and wanted. To know that people were pleased with me had always been the driving force for me, along with the need to be perfect, to be the ultimate people pleaser. I just didn't know it at the time.

Chapter 2

All the Firsts

It's been fourteen days since I last had a drink. The cravings and the anxiety are definitely still there. But my body feels different. It seems to have suddenly remembered how much sleep affects everything else, from my mood to my digestion to my anxiety. Now that I have adopted a better sleeping rhythm and am not waking up at three in the morning with the room spinning and feeling like I haven't had a drink of water in years, I feel like a different person. I've been doing a lot of reading. There's a ton of scientific research behind what alcohol does to your body, and more specifically to your sleep. If I had only known this before I ever started. Well, to be honest, I probably still would have embarked on my unhealthy relationship with alcohol, but at least I could have said I knew better.

Anyhow, fourteen days. And the silence of sobriety, the way my thoughts can fill the space like they haven't in a very long time has been eye-opening—before, with the drinks, I was actively trying to numb any and every thought and I was just living like a robot. Writing has always been a form of therapeutic expression for me. Writing has facilitated the formulation of my thoughts in a way that has helped keep myself honest about my feelings or at least aware of them. I have a habit of relying on handwritten checklists and pros-

and-cons lists. I distinctly remember making checklists every single day before college, writing out the things I needed to do that day, and I felt so much accomplishment and joy when all the things were checked off at the end of the day. Now that I'm taking a step back and really seeing things clearly, I know a lot needs to change in order for me to really put one hundred percent effort into living a life full of passion and purpose for the second half of my life. And it starts with me. It is nobody else's job to fill up my cup. I need to fill up my cup first before I worry that others are happy and fulfilled. It's like flight attendants prime you as the plane takes off, "put your mask on before you help someone else with theirs." As a parent, that's so fucking hard. You want to make sure your kids are taken care of before you are. But the reality is, if I am deprived of oxygen and pass out because of it, I cannot take care of another. How well can I take care of someone else if I can't take care of myself first?

In my junior year of high school, I promptly learned not to take care of myself. When I fell in love for the first time, I had absolutely no concern for my own well-being. I only cared that the object of my obsession was happy. Before I met Christopher[*], I had crushes on boys, but I hadn't ever experienced the physical pull to be near someone quite like I did with him. From the beginning, I felt the need to make sure he was happy, even while my happiness was usually at the bottom of his list of priorities. When I think back to this time, my first thought is to make sure my own kids don't experience what I did. But then I stop myself, because maybe that's their journey. And, if it is, if heartbreak and the all-encompassing obsession of first love and first heartbreak is what's in their story, then I'll be there to support them however they let me. I hope and pray that's not their story, but, if it is, we'll all survive. I did.

Another important aspect about HSPs is that we love hard. We fall hard and fast, and our love is on a different level, because we feel

---

[*] Some names in this story have been changed for privacy reasons.

things so deeply. But, as Elaine Aron writes, it's incredibly difficult for a non-HSP to return that level of love. She says, "Extremely intense love is often rejected by the beloved just because it is so demanding and unrealistic."[5] Maybe my love was too much for him.

Maybe it overwhelmed and made unrealistic demands of him. But neither of us knew it at the time.

Everything about that first relationship was intense. We went to a small Christian high school, so everybody knew everyone else's business at all times. I was the new girl, and suddenly, one of the most popular boys in the school was interested in me. I was informed by pretty much every girl in my grade and the grades surrounding mine that he was the one nobody else was going to get to date, because he'd been in a relationship the year prior that basically made him unable to commit to anyone else. Despite the many warnings from Sarah and my new friends, I quickly became infatuated with him, and a few weeks into the school year, he asked me to be his date to Homecoming. It was my first school dance, and I was terrified. The whole process was new to me; finding a dress, wearing footwear that wasn't soccer cleats or tennis shoes, getting my hair done and putting makeup on. The dance ended, and one of my new friends was having a little "after dance movie night" at her house. Up until that point, we had only held hands and slow danced (which I was terrible at—and that hasn't changed over the years). After the movie, the boys all had to leave, and the girls were sleeping over at my friend's house. I drove Christopher to his house down the street, and when I dropped him off, he pulled me out of the car and kissed me. It wasn't anything like the awkward moment I was expecting. It was pretty perfect, actually.

Looking back, I can recognize and accept that I have an addictive personality. And most of the addictions I've encountered along the way have either felt good physically or been meant to punish me physically. Soccer for instance, good. Cutting and self-injury,

5   Aron, Elaine. *The Highly Sensitive Person*, Kensington Publishing Corp, 1996, 141.

punitive. Kissing this boy became a new addiction. I couldn't get enough of being near him, and this boy wanting to be near me was intoxicating for me. I wanted more all the time. Shortly after Homecoming, Christopher decided he was interested in his ex-girlfriend again, and he put the brakes on our relationship. I was upset, but I think I was still in the infatuation stage, so my emotions hadn't gotten to the point where I was devastated by this breakup. In hindsight, I think the split was a good thing, because I'd discovered something that made me feel a huge dopamine rush (attention from boys) and now I was free to explore that experience a little bit with some new friends.

For a few months, I went on a series of bad decision-making tours. Making out with a friend's ex-boyfriend in a movie theater. And then again at his house. And then again behind the building at school. And then finding out that he wasn't her ex-boyfriend after all. She'd just gone out of town and was angry with him, so he figured he'd tell people they broke up because this was before the time of cell phones and texting twenty-four seven. Another bad decision named Drew showed up around this time. He was Chrisopher's best friend. I got into this weird game of cat-and-mouse with Drew for months. I fell for Drew before he could really "chase" me and following our first encounter it became a back-and-forth with him. He was different than Christopher though. He was different than the friend's ex-boyfriend. He was different than any boy or man I've met since then. He'll always be someone that I think of with the fond memories of being held as if he didn't ever want to let go, and being kissed like he had all the time in the world to do nothing else. He made me feel like I was special, and, to be fair, he also made a lot of other girls feel that way. A charmer, and a kind soul, even if he didn't always want to share that latter attribute with the rest of the world. He was one of the good ones for me.

My first experience with drinking occurred when I was sixteen years old, and it was a disaster. My older sister and her boyfriend took me and my friend (sometimes enemy) Brittany[*] to their friend's house, where the parents were either too old to notice the under-age drinking or passed out drunk themselves. I vaguely remembe speaking to an older man who seemed comfortable with a bunch of teenagers, including a couple of us well under the age of eighteen, drinking and smoking weed in his house. Most of that night was an absolute blur. I can now identify that I was a blackout drinker from that first night. Of course, now I know more about drinking behaviors from my sobriety studies, but I didn't know at the time that most blackout drinkers start that way, and that's the only way they learn how to drink. Drink until nothing else matters. Drink until the pain stops, until all you feel is the buzz. And then you feel nothing because you stepped over the line of consciousness.

I drank a lot of beer that night. I never drank beer again after that night. To my recollection, I had a couple beers and then just kept going and was told after the fact that I was throwing up and had to be pulled to my bed when my sister and her boyfriend dropped me off at my parents' house later that night. I remember feeling really terrible the next day, in the first of many horrific hangovers. I was also told by Brittany that I was kissing some random guy at the house party, a fact that I had absolutely no memory of, the following day. That was pretty scary for me, but I brushed it off as my first drinking experience, and tried not to dwell on the failures of that night too much. I'd learn later on that one of the things I crave when I'm drinking is a warm body. I'm not particularly picky about who it is, as long as someone is there to fill the void if the alcohol is starting to wear off.

But the thing that I heard people saying after that first night of drinking was how funny I was, and how friendly I was with the guys who were at the house. Later on, as drinking became a habit for me, I heard from friends that I was someone people wanted to be around, until I wasn't. There was another, darker side that came out when I drank, even from these first experiences. At some point, after a handful of drinks, I became antagonistic toward everyone I was close to. I kept poking at my sister and her boyfriend and Brittany, just to get a reaction out of someone. But despite how crappy I felt the next day

17

and the fact that I couldn't remember eighty percent of the night, it didn't matter as much as feeling like people liked me when I was drinking. I didn't drink for a while after that first time, but it wasn't intentional—alcohol just wasn't readily available to me like it was that night. I settled back into my sometimes-good-girl Christian school persona, and sometimes-meeting-boys in dark photography rooms or movie theater hallways. No matter which one showed up, I was always open to the next thing or person that would make me feel something, even if those feelings were fleeting.

I was constantly conflicted. I didn't know how to not be a good girl, but I felt this yearning deep inside that there was something more out there for me. Turning to Glennon Doyle once again, I quote: "When we are little girls, our families, teachers, and peers insist that our loud voices, bold opinions and strong feelings are 'too much' and unladylike, so we learn to not trust our personalities. Childhood stories promise us that girls who dare to leave the path or explore get attacked by big bad wolves and pricked by deadly spindles, so we learn to not trust our curiosity. The beauty industry convinces us that our thighs, frizz, skin, fingernails, lips, eyelashes, leg hair, and wrinkles are repulsive and must be covered and manipulated, so we learn to not trust the bodies we live in."[6]

I didn't trust my body or my personality when I was a teenager. My body was something that I could use to my advantage at times, but it was also my target when I needed to feel pain or take out some of my anger on something tangible. I would use myself as a pincushion when things weren't going the way they were supposed to in my perfectionist mind. I didn't learn to trust myself, my body, or my personality until very recently, into my forties. At this time in my life, the purpose of my body and my personality were to make someone else happy, never myself. I would carry this conviction into my first marriage, into my second marriage, and only very recently learned to reconsider and reverse it for my benefit. My new goal was to take my own power back, and to protect my peace above all other

---

6   Doyle, Glennon. *Untamed*, New York:,The Dial Press, 2020, 115.

things. To acknowledge that my personality isn't something I need to turn on and off to make others around me comfortable. That my body isn't a weapon, or something to abuse (from someone else's hands or my own).

Christopher came back around after he saw that other people wanted to hang out with me. I'm still not entirely sure how much he knew about my connection with Drew in the months between Homecoming and the spring of my junior year of high school. But it was enough for him to make an effort and start talking to me again, especially after his ex-girlfriend dropped him. This was a recurring pattern with Christopher—he couldn't be alone, and if it wasn't me or his ex-girlfriend he needed to be with, it was always someone, anyone. There was the girl he took to Winter Formal because I turned him down, not wanting to get back together with him when I was playing my cat-and-mouse game with Drew. It was Brittany before I came to the school, and it was a coworker or a friend of a friend years down the road. Christopher was codependent and needed others to fill his bucket, which I just didn't realize at the time. And with me as an HSP with compulsive and addictive tendencies, we were trouble from the onset. Two kids with unresolved issues, we were trying to find something in each other to heal the broken parts of us. Now that I can look back at our relationship and patterns with a clearer view, I can see that we were both way too immature and unhealthy in our relationships with ourselves to ever make it work as a couple. But no one could say we didn't try.

Another activity that I'd taken a keen interest in during the time Christopher and I were apart my junior year is actively choosing not to eat. I have a history of disordered eating, as far back as junior high school, when I can remember skipping breakfast, eating a bag of chips for lunch, and saying I ate too much after school to want dinner. Again, my body was a weapon that I could use to my advantage. You want to be thinner than the other girls in eighth grade? Stop eating. The perfectionist tendencies ran strong throughout my childhood, and I can remember cutting photos out of magazines and creating these huge scrapbooks and binders full of collages of the celebrities and pro athletes I aspired to look like. Making those collages was one of my main hobbies as a pre-teen and it allowed me to build a vision board of sorts, which showed how I wanted to portray myself to the rest of the world. In 2024, social media influences our teenagers' body image; back then, it was the teen magazines and images of celebrities that we idolized that affected us.

I think I was down to an unhealthy 105 pounds by the time Junior Prom rolled around. I was playing two sports year-round, with my soccer team outside of school ranking as top priority, and then playing volleyball, softball, and soccer at my small private school as a secondary priority. I had to play on the boys' varsity soccer team because there wasn't a girls soccer team there. It was three other girls and me on the team, and boy, did I love the attention from the guys in that group. Because I was one of only a few girls on the team, there was never a time when I didn't have someone's attention on the bus to and from games or during practices. It honestly didn't matter if the guy who was paying attention to me had a girlfriend, was cute, or was rude. I reveled in the attention, even if it came from the wrong people (like someone else's boyfriend). My need to please people and my fear of disappointing people has led to codependency in friendships and romantic relationships. It has also driven me to actively try to avoid making people upset, even at my own expense sometimes.

Chapter 3

High School Hypocrisy

Christopher, my Homecoming date, became my boyfriend sometime before Prom of my junior year. My high school dance date would remain the same for my entire senior year, as we became a "solid" couple around the time of Junior Prom and stayed that way until we divorced almost exactly ten years after I met him. Even though I knew our relationship wasn't perfect, once I committed to being in that relationship with Christopher, I had him as my top priority. I wanted him to be glad that he chose me, and I did everything in my power to make sure I looked the part of the girlfriend he wanted by his side. Every single first was with him. My happiness, my self-worth, my feeling like I was enough were all wrapped up in him. It was crushing to hear girls at school say he was flirting with other people. He had been rumored to do more than flirting for large chunks of our relationship. I couldn't control his actions, but I could control how I presented myself in the role of picture-perfect girlfriend.

I had a few amazing friends during this time. Sarah was my rock. She was often the one person who tethered me back to reality, the one who showed me love, even when I was an asshole to her because my entire focus was on Christopher. Sarah had another good friend she had known since childhood, who became one of my closest friends and I still call a friend to this day, almost twenty-five years later. We'll call her Laura.[*] Laura introduced herself to me in a way that is so typical of her personality. Thinking about the way Laura handled it still makes me smile. On the first day of school, she walked over to me, gave me a hug, and said, "Hi, I'm Laura. Sarah and I have been best friends since we were babies. And now, me and you are going to be best friends!"

Sarah and Laura—they were the angels on my shoulder for my junior and senior years of high school. They had boyfriends as well, but weren't moving nearly as fast as I was in the physical intimacy department. I know their religious beliefs influenced their choices, but maybe they also recognized that they just weren't ready for that kind of emotional attachment to another human being. I can tell you that I probably wasn't ready either, but my need to be loved and desired outweighed the warnings from anyone telling me to slow down and not give in quite so quickly. Without Sarah and Laura, who knows where I would have ended up. I'm grateful to them for not only reminding me that I was worth more than giving my body and soul to a guy that I barely trusted to stay faithful to me most days, but also that I was loved no matter what decisions I made in my romantic relationship. They were and are the definition of true friends, through and through.

Sarah and Laura didn't drink in high school. Christopher drank when it was available to him, but I wouldn't classify him as a heavy drinker by any means. We didn't drink together during high school, or go to insane parties. Christopher and I had an unhealthy addiction to being around each other and would often be reprimanded by school staff, because we were too close or too touchy or too affectionate with each other during the school day. It's embar rassing to think of the many times we were fooling around in the back of someone else's car on the way to school sporting events. We were uncontrollable in our need to constantly be filling each other's space.

---

[*] Some names in this story have been changed for privacy reasons.

Over the summer between my junior and senior year, Christopher replaced alcohol as a bad habit. I spent all of my free time either with him, or playing soccer, or hanging out with friends. I started to pull away from Sarah and Laura's crowd a bit as we entered senior year. They were hosting Bible studies, and I was sneaking out of class to meet up with Christopher. He and I pushed our physical relationship a little further each and every time we were together, and by the first few months of my senior year, we were having sex. I was seventeen when I lost my virginity to the man who would become my first husband. I can't say that I regret that, because so much of our story is wrapped up in our firsts together, and the end result of our relationship was two beautiful children. So, I will never be sad or angry that he was in my life because of that simple fact. I can be sad and angry about things he did and the way he treated me, and our kids, but I'm not ever going to regret that our stories intertwined. We were meant to be what we were to each other, and I'm grateful for that part of our story. I got the best pieces of him. Not only did I know and love him before drugs destroyed his life, but I get to see the absolute BEST parts of him every single day in my twins.

As Christopher and I hung out less with my friends and their "good-kid" crowd, we started hanging out a little bit more with other couples and troublemaker kids who drank and did drugs. They were most likely students at the Christian school only because they had been expelled from their local public school. In this group, we found opportunities to drink and be reckless. We had water bottles filled up with vodka in the limo on the way to Senior Prom. Christopher and his best friends would smoke cigarettes in the parking lot down the street from our school, and they would race their cars down quiet neighborhood streets. Stupid teenage stuff. Senior Prom was a fun night, and it ended, of course, with an after-party at the house of a friend of Christopher's whose parents were never around. Christopher and I spent a lot of time that night trying to find a room we could lock so that we could have some alone time. Some of my memories from that time are so sweet. Some are still painful to this day.

Sarah and Laura were at that same party and found out about my activities behind closed doors with Christopher. They told their parents, who then told my parents, and I was removed from the list of attendees for our softball team's tournament to Catalina Island that month. I was absolutely devastated. Christopher was on the baseball team, and I was on the softball team, and both teams were going to Catalina for this tournament with chaperones. I was also pulled into a meeting at school with the principal and school secretary (who happened to be Laura's mom) to be counseled about premarital sex. It was awkward and humiliating and made me feel like I was broken and disgusting. It was one of the most painful experiences of my life, for two reasons. First, I felt betrayed in so many different ways by people I loved and trusted, and, second, I was being shamed for something that I knew half of the kids on that campus were doing. It was so hypocritical and skewed my opinion of religion for a long time to come.

Around this same time, two friends and schoolmates of mine found out they were pregnant. One was kicked out of the Christian school because her boyfriend didn't attend the same high school, and they couldn't have a pregnant girl walking around "influencing" the rest of us to do the same. The other had a mysteriously timed miscarriage and was able to return to school. Her boyfriend is the one I made out with in the movie theater when he had told me they broke up over Christmas break (a real winner, that one), and he did attend our school. He never faced any consequences. He wasn't asked to leave the school, wasn't kicked off the football or baseball team. No consequences. Talk about double standards.

Chapter 4

The Shattering

There was a lot of chaos the summer between my senior year and my first year of college. I spent most of my time working a part-time job or with Christopher and his group of friends. I rarely drank that summer, and enjoyed going to concerts, watching movies, and spending evenings at the beach around bonfires with friends. I was going to be attending a local state university that August. Christopher had decided school wasn't for him and he was working with a friend of his dad's, at his company. Christopher would come over during the summer while my parents were at work (thank goodness my generation didn't have to worry about Ring cameras) and we'd hang out. He was restless and I could tell that he was getting bored with our relationship. He had started spending time with a group of friends that summer, which included some older girls, and they went to dance clubs. In the meantime, I was really focused on my college classes. I could sense us drifting apart, and, by the time I finished my finals, during my first semester of college, I knew the writing was on the wall. He had probably already cheated on me with at least one of the older girls in that new group of friends. He broke it off with me in December, saying he needed to date around before settling down. This pattern was repeated with Christopher over and over again, even after so many handwritten promises from him in my high school yearbook that we were each other's forever. I was absolutely shattered.

The shattering for me at this time of my life came with physical pain that I chose to inflict on myself. I had been cutting since I was thirteen years old, with no end in sight. The evening that Christopher told me we were done is one of the most vivid memories of my life. I took out the sadness I felt inside through the coping mechanism most familiar to me and carved into my skin. I know that a lot of people, even those who love me, don't understand the behavior of cutting or any form of self-injury. The night that cutting changed my life was December 30, 2000. I was sitting on the floor of my bathroom, following a heated discussion with Christopher about getting back together—after he'd dropped me for the older girl he had been hooking up with for the past few weeks. Christopher hadn't actually volunteered the news, his best friend, Josh[*] had. Josh and I had been close since senior year, and he was one of my best friends at this point too. I appreciated him always telling me the truth and looking out for me, even while he was Christopher's friend. Josh was definitely one of the good ones. In an alternate universe, maybe I would have ended up with him and my life would have been vastly different. But that's not the story I wrote for myself.

That night, just before the New Year of 2001, when I should have been enjoying my first year of college and having fun with my friends, I was battling with myself about whether or not Christopher was my happily-ever-after. A couple of hours went by, and I lost the emotional struggle. I decided to take the pain into my own hands, instead of letting the emotional torment pull me on this roller coaster again and again. I pulled out a razor blade that I had kept hidden in my bathroom drawer, and started carving into my arms. My lower arms had been the site of cutting before, with small marks resembling puppy or kitten scratches that I could cover up

---

[*] Some names in this story have been changed for privacy reasons.

with long sleeves and that healed up in a few days with enough Neosporin. This time, I reached for the fleshy skin on the inside of my upper arm, and I sliced way too deep. The gash ripped across my skin, about half an inch across and I was scared that I'd done something I couldn't cover up with long sleeves and bandages. Blood started oozing out of my arm and I screamed. My mom came rushing into my room when she heard the scream, and she pounded on the bathroom door. I started to get light-headed as I looked at the blood gathering under my arm on the bathroom floor. This was it, I thought. I'm going to die here on the bathroom floor and everyone's going to think I tried to kill myself.

Self-injury is something that is difficult to understand. It was portrayed most powerfully in a movie called Thirteen, starring Nikki Reed and Evan Rachel Wood. Any other depictions I've seen of self-injury in the media have been difficult for me to watch. I don't feel like the story is told correctly. It angers me to see the way others cringe or make a joke out of those who cut themselves, representing them as desperate for attention and wanting to make people feel sorry for them. Self-injury is too punishing a practice to be a mere mechanism for attention seeking. The best way I can describe the feeling at the root of this practice is that you are truly shattered to your core. And to make that inward pain something that you can control, you bring the pain to the surface.

I opened the door to the bathroom and my mom just kept asking over and over again, "What are you doing? Why did you do this?" I was freaked out by seeing my own blood in a volume larger than I had witnessed before. I was also frantic because of an emotional high I couldn't come down from, after all the back and forth with Christopher. My dad came in a second later and just started muttering under his breath. Looking back, I think he was trying to fix it, and he started to pull me up and say he was taking me to the hospital. My mom calmed him down, saying that it would be fine. She started to apply Neosporin on my arm and bandage it up with gauze. My siblings popped in and out, possibly traumatized by that night too. After a while, I was calm and tired enough to go to bed. My mom sat on the floor in front of my bed, just stroking my uncut arm, over and over again, until I fell asleep. That night, I slept fitfully. I can now liken that sleep to that drunken slumber, where you actually get no rest at all, and are just in limbo for hours on end. I kept dreaming that I was falling, and I woke up to my own tears a few times that night. I felt broken, and I was scared for what was to come. I was terrified of how my parents would respond to this. And I was so mad that my self-injury was now known.

I had ruined it. My secret was out. People could perceive cracks in the surface, and could not see the good-girl Christian valedictorian I could have been, nor the strong girl who didn't care if Christopher had moved on. I wasn't projecting the perfectionist image that I so desired to display. I was caught in a situation where I had to figure out what path I took next. Was I going to jump in headfirst with Christopher and close my eyes to the bad things in our relationship, just to prove that I could make this work? That I could fix this? The perfectionist in me knew I needed to do something to rewrite the story I had told that night. I needed to prove to everyone that I was in control, that things were fine, and that I wasn't broken.

Chapter 5

Moving On Out

When I was eighteen years old, I moved out of my parents' house. I decided that if I wanted to be with Christopher, we needed more time to spend together. According to Christopher, his mom offered to let me move into their house for a couple weeks to sort out what my next steps would be. It was a really tumultuous time period for me and my family. My parents were heartbroken that I was making decisions they didn't agree with, and my sister was livid. My little brothers were sad that I was leaving, but they mostly stayed out of the line of fire during that time. I'm eight years older than my little brothers, so there was always a little bit of a divide between us, growing up: the girls (my sister and me) and the boys.

My sister and I have had a complicated relationship as far back as I can remember. I've always wanted to be just like my older sister. We'd play with the neighborhood kids in our huge front yard on Monterey Street, and I would watch her every move. When she was in eighth grade and I was in sixth grade, a friend of hers invited me to go hang out with them after school. My sister absolutely lost her shit. She threw a fit in the middle of the school parking lot because the worst thing imaginable would be for her nerdy little sister to tag along. Later in high school, she would try to get me to hang out with some of her guy friends. But, at that point, I didn't trust that she had good intentions, and I kept mostly to myself when we were going to the same high school my freshman and sophomore years. I have a vivid memory of my sister trying to choke me in the back of our family minivan, while my dad went inside to pick up my foster brother for the weekend. I was probably nine or ten years old at the time. I have another powerful recollection of my sister sitting on top of my chest choking me before I left my parents' house that day. I've never truly known if she's capable of loving me in the way that I needed her to love me. Later on, watching her become a mom, I saw some really good qualities in her. We just aren't built the same, and that's OK. But there were traumatic experiences between her and me growing up. These events gave rise to a boundary that I must keep intact in order to protect myself and my peace as I become who I'm supposed to be in this life. Not every family relationship is perfect, and ours is definitely one that has known ups and downs along our journey. I'll always want her to be happy and healthy, but sometimes, protecting my happiness and health means maintaining boundaries for myself with people I love. And that's OK.

Leaving my parent's house that day was one of the hardest things I have ever done. I left while my dad was at work, because I knew I couldn't face the disappointment on his face when he heard about my decision. As I left, I knew that I was breaking my mom's heart. I was also terrified of not making it down the street before my dad got home, because I knew seeing him would break what little resolve I had at that point. When Christopher arrived at my parents' house to pick me up, I looked at him, my eyes brimming with tears, and got into his truck. I cried all the way to his mom's house, and I couldn't talk to anyone that entire night. Christopher came into the guest room where I was staying at his mom's house, and sat with me while we watched a movie. But he was also still entertaining a few of his friends who had migrated over to the house as well. I stayed in that room, just kind of in a daze about my decision to leave, and to no longer be that good girl who listened to her parents and made decisions based on what others thought was best. I had made a decision for myself—as terrible as it may have been—and I followed through with it. Those few weeks where I stayed with Christopher's mom, and then with an old friend from high school who was looking for a roommate, were chaotic and stressful for me. I still worked a part-time job near the college I was attending, so I had a little bit of income to help pay for groceries and rent, but it wasn't much. After I had lived a couple weeks with this friend, Christopher's mom said that she would help us get into an apartment by the college, as long as we both continued working and I stayed in school. She knew that my plans involved having a college degree, and, even though she and I didn't always agree, I knew that she fully supported me in that endeavor.

Christopher became my security blanket when I no longer had my family to fall back on, because I had pushed them away. I blindly accepted my new life as a college student living with her boyfriend in a tiny one-bedroom apartment, surviving on macaroni and cheese and cereal. In June 2001, I turned nineteen years old. Two weeks after my birthday, Christopher said he had a surprise for me and wanted to take me somewhere. We drove down to a secluded part of the beach, where the waves lapped against rocks and small caves had been carved out by the water's touch over the years. As we walked down the beach, hand in hand, I felt like something big was about to happen. I had told Christopher over the past few months that I wanted to get married, because I felt guilty living together, and why postpone the inevitable? I stupidly believed that we were destined to be together forever, so why not get married now and spend the rest of our lives in happily-ever-after land (while ridding myself of the guilt of living in sin before marriage). That good-girl mentality may have been pushed deep under the surface, but it was always lingering, ready to pop out anytime I needed a good kick to the conscience. That day on the beach, neither of us were saying very much, and I was holding my breath, thinking I might know what was about to happen but not being exactly sure. After we had walked along the beach for a while, Christopher grabbed both of my hands and got down on one knee and said, "I love you, Jenn. And I'm always going to love you. Will you marry me?"

In the charismatic way I knew him to be capable of, he blew me away with those few words. He was so sure of himself, so confident that this was the right thing, that I couldn't possibly see any alternative. I nodded my head, tears filling my eyes, as he slipped a small engagement ring on my finger, the tiny center stone sparkling in the light from the sun that bounced off the water. That day was one that will forever be etched into my memory. It was one of the good days, one of the days that I saw love and innocence and kindness in his eyes. That June afternoon, I was engaged at the ripe old age of nineteen.

Chapter 6:

Living the College Dream

I was so excited to start college. I had dreamed of chasing after my academic goals and having the love of my life all at the same time (shout out to Felicity Porter for inspiring that fairytale dream). My first year of college was mostly uneventful, aside from the between-semester drama with Christopher. I was a good student. I majored in something new each semester (I did this for a couple years) and I loved the learning environment. I could envision myself doing this for years and years. So, it's no surprise that, at some point during my undergraduate degree, I decided to pursue a graduate degree with the goal of becoming a college professor myself one day.

Unfortunately, the personal turmoil I was experiencing when I started my sophomore year at a local California State University led to my first really intense, identifiable panic attack. This episode resulted in my automatically dropping out of all my classes, and declaring myself (the high school valedictorian, mind you) a college failure. I remember sitting in a chair in my chemistry lab and my mind just started spinning. A thousand unintelligible thoughts swirled around, my hands started to sweat, my heart began racing, and I felt like someone was choking me. I had no idea what was going on, I just knew that I had to get out of there.

That evening, Christopher found me sitting on our tiny apartment couch in a ball, my body swaddled in a blanket. I was just staring at the walls, in the dark. A complete mess. I felt like I had no direction, and like I was going crazy. I wish mental health was something we talked about back then, in the early 2000s. It just wasn't something you would casually bring up, and going to therapy wasn't for "normal" people. It was a different time. We were all supposed to be capable and able to fix our flaws as quietly as possible.

When I think back to earlier times of stress as a kid or teenager, I think panic and anxiety were always a part of my reality. I just didn't know how to name it at that time. In addition, as an HSP, I felt further pain as a result of this panic attack because it didn't just affect me. The disappointment and worry felt by my parents and friends overwhelmed me. I think that, at that point, I really became unabashedly codependent with Christopher. Regardless of how badly he treated me, how many times he cheated, I would always stay with him. Because he helped me in that moment of complete despair—he was kind to me, reassuring. And no matter what has happened between us in the past two decades, I will always be thankful for the compassion that he showed in my weaker moments, my days where the struggle with my mental health crippled me.

Almost immediately after I dropped all my classes, I regretted it. I was working part-time as an office manager, so I picked up extra hours. I also set my sights on becoming a domestic goddess, ramping up my cleaning skills in our tiny apartment. And I watched way too much television, while Christopher spent most of his time out of the house with friends.

After my skipped first semester of sophomore year, I became fully committed to the completion of my degree, because I loved college. So, I decided to double up on classes, so that I could catch up and get my bachelor's degree a semester early. I took a full-time load of classes at a local community college, while taking a full-time load of classes at the university for two semesters, and threw in a couple of summer and intersession classes for good measure. As a now forty-something woman with teenagers, I always tell them and their friends to enjoy every minute of college, if they decide to go. I encourage my kids to go away and live that college life, and experience the independence. If I have one big regret in life, it's choosing to stay local and go to college (largely because of Christopher at the time) as a commuter. Aside from that aspect, I enjoyed my college experience very much. After I graduated with my bachelor's degree in American Studies in January 2004, I enrolled in a graduate program right away. When I set my mind to something (good or bad), I can get shit done. I finished my undergraduate degree in three years and went on to finish my graduate courses in two years, putting the final piece of my thesis on hold when I had the twins. With unhealthy habits too I go all-in. The compulsion to be perfect and to do things well leaves no time for me to slow down and go easy on things.

Some of my greatest memories are still of moments in college where an engaging conversation in a classroom sparked my interest in a new area of study. I loved getting lost in the work on a research paper or dabbling in various disciplines. I changed my major about six times, but the one thing that carried through my entire collegiate experience was the love of learning and being challenged by classmates or professors. My desire to become a college professor was sparked by my own experience as a student. I still look up to many of my college professors, who were some of the most influential people in my adult life.

Because I was focused on my college academics, I turned a blind eye to a lot of things that were going on in my personal life and later in my marriage. In the fall of 2001, the whole country was shaken up by the attacks of September 11th. It was a very uneasy time for a lot of us. But I kept my head down, went to school, worked my part-time job. I also didn't question much when Christopher came home late—nor when I stopped by his work one day and found him in a back room with a female coworker in a compromising position. I swallowed up his lies because I didn't want to admit that I might have chosen wrong. Choosing him might have been the wrong choice, but I couldn't change that now. What I could control were my grades in school and my success there. So the perfectionist people pleaser in me decided to focus on school. I didn't party in college. Married at nineteen, I lived a very different life than most college students. And that was OK as long as I had good grades and a bright future ahead of me. Christopher was part of that picture in my head, but there were cracks showing on the surface of that picture-perfect relationship from the very beginning.

My first wedding was a sad day. My parents were trying to show up for me and be supportive, but their nineteen-year-old daughter was marrying a kid they didn't think was all that wonderful, and Christopher's mom didn't even bother to show up. We didn't have any of our friends there because we decided to get married in Las Vegas, and none of our friends were even twenty-one years old. It was a really depressing day when it should have been a day of celebration and love and joy. When I look back at pictures of that day, it breaks my heart. There were some people in our lives who were genuinely happy for us and supported us, but this hasty wedding was not a solid foundation to start a marriage. Neither of us was emotionally, mentally, or financially ready for that step. My face in those pictures reflected how scared I felt and revealed how worried I was about what other people were thinking and feeling.

And then there was my sister. She and her boyfriend decided to get engaged the weekend of my wedding. She often would not allow me to have the spotlight, which I had struggled with throughout my childhood. Scheduling her engagement at that time is another example of her constant need to be the center of attention. I continue to grapple with that, to this day. She can get quietly jealous of my relationship with my parents, and has seemed conflicted in recent years with my relationship with her daughters.

The year that I finished my undergraduate degree, my sister had her first child. I had a brand-new niece whom I adored, and another one was on the way. Christopher was up to his old tricks, and I was choosing to look the other way. I heard rumors all the time of Christopher hooking up with random girls from work, or girls he met through new friends he made at work, or riding dirt bikes, or golfing, or going to the local casinos. There was always a lie that covered up whatever shenanigans he was up to, and I think I just started to accept that I wasn't worthy of a loving, faithful relationship. I should be happy I "got" the guy that everyone else wanted to date in high school. I should be happy to settle for whatever scrap of love and attention he showed to me at any given time. I started to gain weight, and that was difficult for me. My self-worth since I met Christopher had been wrapped up in my appearance, and how much attention he showed me. As I started to gain weight, I didn't find that Christopher and I had as strong a physical connection as we used to. I could tell that he was more interested in thinner, more edgy girls he met at his work. So, I shifted my attention to being the best aunt to my new baby nieces that I could be. Becoming the perfect aunt, sacrificing my sleep and relationships with friends and my husband to make sure I was always there for my sister and her girls were a new avenue to reach perfection. Thus, I could be good and helpful, just as I had always learned I should be—a good girl who didn't make waves or stir up any trouble.

In early December 2005, I found out that I was pregnant. I was so happy. I wanted to be a mom more than anything now that I had this deep connection with my nieces. I wanted my kids to be of comparable age to my nieces so that they could all grow up close. My sister and I had two cousins whom we grew up to be really attached to, and I wanted my kids to experience that bond. About a week after finding out I was pregnant, I suffered a miscarriage. I was devastated. With that loss, I felt like I had failed. Something must be wrong with my body that I wasn't able to carry this baby to term. It was my fault. Taking this mentality into a Christmas party with friends was one of the worst decisions I've ever made. I was heartbroken by this loss, and just wanted to make all the feelings disappear.

Looking back at this event, I realize now how I used alcohol entirely as a numbing agent. I wanted to keep up with the most seasoned drinkers in our friend group. We had become very close with this group of about five or six couples. But that night, I decided I would be one of the guys and match them shot for shot. I was friendly with all of the men in our group, which was acceptable because they were all our friends. But sitting on their laps, flirting, right with their wives and my husband sitting there, was all too strange—beyond strange. I would never be comfortable with that now in my sobriety. I crossed lines with these men that night. My behavior then reflected the deepening foundation of my relationship with alcohol. There was no middle ground for me, no boundary. Once I started, I didn't stop until I blacked out. And that night, the blackout landed me in an emergency room. Returning home in a cab with Christopher the next morning, I felt deep shame. He had stayed with me during that ordeal, but the next day he didn't seem especially concerned. He was visibly more annoyed that I had interrupted his night with his friends and taken away his sleep than he was worried about what was going on with me and my drinking behavior.

Drinking at this time in my life was something I did rarely. But when I did it, I did it big. I had no limits, and I enjoyed feeling the release of not caring anymore what I did or keeping this mask of perfection on. It was an odd combination: committed college graduate student by day, but then girl who drinks herself (nearly) into a coma one night.

A few months after this, I found out I was pregnant again. Christopher and I were on a trip with some of our best friends and my family to Austin, Texas, so that I could check out the doctorate program in American Studies at University of Texas Austin. We were seriously considering moving from Southern California to Austin for this program, and for a change of pace and a lower cost of living. At the time, in early 2006, housing prices in Texas were a fraction of what they were in Southern California. The day before we got on the plane heading to Austin, I took a pregnancy test. Positive tests (a few of them, just to be sure) confirmed that I was pregnant. I called my doctor's office to make an appointment for the next week to find out how far along I was, even though I could make an educated guess, and get the prenatal appointments rolling. I didn't tell anyone that I was pregnant at first, until we went out to dinner and someone asked why I wasn't eating much. I shared that I was suffering from morning sickness, which happened to last all day. I had taken a few tests and they were all positive. Everyone there was very happy for us. It was wonderful to feel loved and supported by my family, and our closest friends at that time. I felt like this pregnancy would give Christopher and me a clean slate to move forward and build our family together. I was happy for what the future could bring. I was cautiously optimistic that this pregnancy would stick, and we'd finally get to live out our happily-ever-after.

Chapter 7

Double Trouble

My first check-up at the doctor was to confirm whether I was in fact pregnant. I went into the doctor's office early in April of 2006. I was scared to death, having recently gone through a miscarriage that ripped my heart out, and seeing all of my friends and family enjoy their "perfect lives" with their "little miracles" running around. Christopher and I waited in the doctor's office for what seemed like an eternity before I was called into an examination room. Dr. Finn* did an exam and then ordered a blood test to find out how much HCG was in my blood levels, which would help determine whether it was a viable pregnancy. Dr. Finn said that, based on the calculations, I was seven weeks pregnant at this point. She said that everything looked good and that her nurse would call with the blood test results in a couple days and we would go from there. I was thrilled that the doctor didn't see any problems, but also terrified that I might lose the baby or that the blood test would come back and show that I wasn't pregnant after all. This constant waiting game to find out if everything was OK was a very scary time for me. I was throwing up just about every five minutes at this point, so I was fairly certain that I was pregnant or else my body was doing a fantastic job of pretending. I was also tired all the time.

---

* Some names in this story have been changed for privacy reasons.

Whie I was at work, I got a phone call from the doctor's office the next afternoon. When I saw the number, I felt terrified. I went outside to take the call. The nurse said that the blood test results came back, and I was pregnant. However, there was something abnormal in the results, so they wanted me to come in for an ultrasound the next week. I asked a few questions, a little panicked but hoping it would all work out. The waiting game continued that week, and I tried to focus on school and work and anything but that doctor's appointment, but it loomed over my head. Time dragged on, and finally, it was ultrasound day. I went into the appointment and prepared myself for the worst. The technician began the ultrasound, with Christopher by my side, holding my hand. My eyes searched wildly across the ultrasound machine screen, trying to figure out if there was something wrong. The ultrasound tech could not tell me anything about what the ultrasound was capturing. It was the doctor's responsibility to do so. I felt like the ultrasound tech kept repeating the same measurements two or perhaps three times. Due to this duplication, I was convinced that something was wrong. What I didn't know at the time and learned later is that the tech repeated the measurements not because something was wrong but because there were two babies, not one. It took about an hour to finish the ultrasound. By the time I got home, I was a sobbing mess. The ultrasound tech had said that my doctor would have the results in the next forty-eight hours, so I had to wait yet again.

Two days later, my phone rang on my way home from the undergraduate course for which I was the teaching assistant, that semester. It was my last semester of coursework for my graduate degree, then I would just have to write my thesis and I'd be done. I had a stack of papers to grade, and was carrying them in the house as I answered the phone call. The nurse on the other end of the line said that she had some very exciting news for me, and I thought, "Oh good, everything's OK with the baby!" Just as I was about to breathe a sigh of relief, the nurse said, "Both babies look wonderful…" She continued to mention something about the measurements, and the fact that I was a little over eight weeks pregnant, which would put my due date on December thirteenth of that year. I had honestly zoned out after she said, "both babies." I was dumbfounded and dropped all my student papers on the ground. I sat down on the stoop of the porch. I waited for the nurse to finish her speech, and then I said very quietly, "I'm sorry. . . . Did you say both babies? As in two babies?" The nurse laughed, and responded, "Yes, that's right. You are pregnant with twins. Congratulations!" I fumbled through a "Thank you" and managed to schedule my next prenatal appointment. I remember hanging up my cell phone and just staring up into space for a few minutes until I picked up the phone to call Christopher. He had a less than enthusiastic response. I told him the news and he freaked out. I was completely hurt by his response. I didn't think this was bad news. Shocking, yes. Overwhelming, absolutely. Financially more of a burden, definitely. But bad news? Two babies couldn't be bad news; it was a miracle to me that I had gotten pregnant with one and had passed the scary eight-week mark. Having two was just double the blessing as far as I was concerned. I was scared, sure, but I figured I would learn as I went and that everything would be just fine. Obviously, it was meant to be or it wouldn't have happened.

I was blessed to have a relatively boring pregnancy up until my eighth month. Sure, I had the regular morning sickness that lasted all-day, but I was working up until the day I went into labor—still hacking away at my graduate degree final project. When I was thirty-four weeks pregnant, I woke up at about three in the morning and discovered that I had either peed my pants (embarrassing) or my water had broken (go-time!). I couldn't quite figure out what the correct answer was, so I decided to take a shower. When it was obvious that the clear liquid was not urine, I woke Christopher up and told him that I thought we should go to the hospital. A few hours later, the water breakage was confirmed, and I was hooked up to several machines. I passed the time with TV and wondered why I never felt those damn contractions like they told me I would. One of the nurses came in and talked to me for a while about the contractions. She couldn't believe I wasn't feeling them. I said that my back was hurting really bad, and that this pain had been pretty constant the past few days. She said that I was having back contractions, and that pretty soon they would start taking over the front side of my belly too. She was right. . . . By noon on November sixth, I could feel the contractions throughout my entire body.

My labor story with the twins is like a lot of women's birth stories up until it wasn't. Because I was having twins, I was wheeled into a surgical room, just in case an emergency C-section was needed. Once the first baby was born, my son, Lucas, I was in panic mode because he wasn't making a sound. They rushed him over to a table where neonatal intensive care unit (NICU) nurses were waiting. They started working on him. After what felt like an eternity, I heard the tiniest little cry come from his body. Seventeen long minutes later, my baby girl was born. Rylee came into the world screaming, and has been loud and full of life ever since.

The doctor said that I only had a minute to hold the twins, laying one on each side of my chest. I stared into their beautiful faces. I remember feeling like my heart was being ripped from my chest when the incubators were hurriedly pushed out of that sterile, brightly lit, cold hospital room. I remember my mom coming into the room and the look in her eyes betrayed her alarm at my appearing to be on the verge of death. Bundles of towels and hospital linens being dumped into a container, while the doctors tried to stop the bleeding. I felt frozen to the core, empty, and scared because they had just taken my babies from me. This wasn't how it was supposed to be. But the twins were almost six weeks early, and needed care in the NICU. I had to trust that the professionals were going to do what they could to help.

After a couple of hours, my teeth had stopped chattering. The doctors had given me some medication to stop the bleeding and forced me to eat and drink before they would let me go to the NICU to see my babies. I remember being wheeled from the maternity ward through the underground tunnel, to the adjoining children's hospital. I saw Lucas hooked up to a ventilator and Rylee wrapped up, all cozy, charming the NICU nurses and looking like the big kid on the block. My heart broke into a million pieces at the sight of my little man not being able to breathe on his own. I wondered if the only thing that was going to save him was my living in that NICU until he was strong enough to leave and go home where all of us belonged. I remember how strong Rylee was from the start, born pink and screaming, while my tiny little four-pound, fourteen-ounce boy struggled to take those first few breaths.

I stayed awake that first night in the hospital, calling the NICU every half hour to make sure my boy was still with us, since I couldn't leave my own hospital room. Rylee looked out of place from the moment she entered that NICU. But within a few days, she was having trouble digesting food and she needed a feeding tube to keep her weight above five pounds (even though she was five pounds fifteen ounces at birth). I watched her get stronger and stronger, and prayed for Lucas to catch up, so that I could take my babies home together. The first time Lucas finished one of those tiny NICU baby bottles, I cried and smiled, and, in that moment, feeling a love for him and Rylee more profound than I ever thought possible. I took my babies home after they spent eleven days in the NICU. Sitting in the back seat between those two infant car seats, I experienced one of the happiest days of my life. I had my babies, they were both safe and thriving, and we were on our way home to start our lives together.

Christopher was in and out of view during the twins' NICU stay. He would see them at least once a day, but I was practically a resident of that NICU. I couldn't stand to be away from them, and I knew that being with them, having them breathe in my scent and feel my heart beating next to theirs, was a proven predictor of their success and growth. In the days to come at home, as I spent nights awake, feeding one baby and then the next, and barely catching thirty minutes of sleep before the next round of feedings, Christopher was next to useless. He wouldn't wake up unless I nudged him HARD, nor did he ever offer to take over any of the duties. But I told myself that I was OK with it. After all, I had wanted to be a mom, and for me that meant I was completely in from the moment they arrived. I had fought to get my babies home, and I would do everything in my power to spend every single second with them.

Those first months with my kids were like nothing I had ever experienced. I fell so incredibly and deeply in love, that I sacrificed everything about myself to make them happy and to be the best mom possible. My purpose and my passion to fulfill that ambition meant numbing my feelings with alcohol was a distant memory. I didn't have any use for that at this point in my life, because being the best mom I could be was all-consuming. My anxiety was mostly under control, except when I felt a little overprotective of who could watch the twins. The list of people whom I trusted to do that was very short.

Christopher was around when it was convenient for him, but overall, his life didn't change all that much. I did the nighttime feedings and I took care of the twins during the day. I also worked full-time from home. My employer had offered me the flexibility to take on a role in human resources and work from home for the first few months after the twins were born. I was happy for the opportunity to be a full-time mom and still have an income. But the boundary between work and home was often blurred, as I found myself working on projects at midnight and doing the babies' nighttime feedings in-between emails and updating employee files. I loved every step of the way, those first nine months. I loved the bonding time of feeding, and I loved watching the twins learn how to eat rice cereal and baby food for the first time. I loved watching them learn how to crawl—Lucas a little bit later than Rylee but chasing after her in no time. I loved being a mom, and I loved my kids beyond belief. I had officially become the crazy mom—entirely devoted to her kids and eating, breathing, and sleeping mommyhood. It was my new focus in life, and I was completely and totally in love.

As happens with most couples when they first start having kids, the dynamic between Christopher and me started to shift. I loved him, and I wanted us to be a happy family, but in my eyes, the twins needed my focus, and he was a grown man, capable of taking care of himself. If he wanted to be a part of their lives or my life, he would have to make the choice to give up his nights out with friends or spend less time gambling at the local casino. His call to make. And boy, did he make it.

Chapter 8

The Decision

When the twins were about nine months old, Christopher and I decided to move nearby to a townhouse. Christopher magically had a work trip scheduled for right before the move, so I was left to handle all of the preparation and logistics for moving day without him, while juggling my job and the twins. He was in Vegas with the new jeweler he was working with. He had started this side gig a few months prior and it had often led to late nights and parties that I wasn't quite on board with. We had been living with my parents since the twins were born, so that we had extra hands to help and we could save up money to get into our own place. Christopher was terrible at managing money, and I usually gave in because fighting him on every spend was exhausting. We were adults with two babies, but very much living like teenagers when it came to making money decisions. But moving into this townhouse was going to be a big deal. Our own place meant our chance to make it a family home for the four of us. I was excited.

Christopher and I spoke a couple times while he was gone, and I was handling all of the last-minute moving details—picking up the keys, dropping off the security deposit and first month's rent, etc. I was thinking that when he got back from Vegas everything would go back to normal. We would put on our happy faces and everything would be just fine. When he got home, he was super affectionate, but I didn't want to have anything to do with him because I had a million things to get done. With Christopher gone on his trip to Vegas, I set all of the plans for moving day, including enlisting the help of friends and family for the day of the move, as well as packing, organizing, and strategizing for the move. Everything was extremely smooth with the move, and at the end of a successful moving day, my friend Sarah helped me set up all of the dishes in the kitchen and put things away while Christopher and the twins went to bed. When Sarah and I were done for the night, I went upstairs and laid down next to my husband, with the babies laying in their cribs next to us, and a torrent of words started pouring out of him. He told me that he couldn't be a full-time husband or a full-time dad because he was too young, and he wanted a different life. I did not know what to say, but I was mad, upset, and hurt, and caught off guard. We went back and forth, me crying and him freaking out and pacing around, saying that he didn't want to hurt me, he didn't want to be a bad dad, didn't want to be a "Disneyland Dad" like his father had been, but that he didn't think he was "living the right life."

What?

I was stunned.

Christopher went on to tell me that maybe he should just be allowed to see other women and be single, while I waited for him to figure it out. That's when I (FINALLY) got angry and defensive of our children. I packed their diaper bag, and then put the twins in their car seats. I told Christopher that I would never let my kids be a "choice" for him, that he either wanted to be part of this family or he didn't. Waiting around for him, while he went and "figured out" what he wanted, wasn't an option. I left my husband standing on the front lawn of the townhouse. That place was supposed to be our new home and yet we hadn't spent even one full night in it as a family. My kids were packed safely in the car and it was about midnight. I called my parents and told them I was driving to their house. I shared that

Christopher had said he didn't want to be married or be a dad anymore. When I left that night, I had no idea what was going to happen to my marriage. Our friends and family had busted their asses to pack up all of our belongings and move them into our new home. And my husband had come home from a weekend adventure in Vegas and decided not to mention to anyone that entire day that he "wanted a new life." I felt angry, crushed, worried, and lost. But my kids had made me a stronger woman, because I fought the urge to control the pain, the hurt, the anger, and the feeling of complete despair. When I got to my parents' house that night, I cried and held my babies and just tried to figure out where the hell I was going to go from here.

Chapter 9

Divorce & Heart Surgery

D ivorce is messy. It's painful.

Christopher had met a stripper in Las Vegas who tickled his fancy more than I, with twin babies at home, did, and he decided that he wanted the flashy lifestyle of clothes, jewelry, drinks, and gambling. His new lady friend was accustomed to those "finer" things in life as well. According to a friend, Christopher shared that when he got home and was jolted back to reality just long enough to let our friends and family move all of our belongings across town into our new townhouse, he couldn't imagine going back into that boring everyday routine. So, he spoke up and broke our family apart. Today, I'm grateful for his decision. If he hadn't made the choices he did, I wouldn't be where I am today. I wouldn't be in a healthy marriage with two more beautiful children and a life I am grateful for every day. I got the best pieces of Christopher in the form of Lucas and Rylee. Who he has become since the night he announced he was no longer involved in our marriage or fatherhood is a person I don't recognize anymore. The person I fell in love with in high school, even if my feelings amounted to blind stupid puppy love, is gone. I see glimpses of him in my daughter's charismatic personality and big laugh. I see him in Lucas's face and in his eyes, and in that impulsive personality and stunning charm. These parts of Christopher's were good and pure and they have been passed down to my two babies, who are now almost adults themselves.

Within a matter of days after moving day (in and out for me and the twins), I had removed myself from the lease at the townhouse. In that time, Christopher had one of his friends and his new girlfriend move into that space, before the ink had even dried on the paperwork starting our divorce proceedings. The twins and I moved back in with my parents, so that I could save money to get into my own place with the twins as soon as possible. I filed for divorce in September 2007, about a month after the move, and Christopher was served with divorce papers within a week of the filing. By November, most of his family had marked me as the devil, claiming that I was keeping the kids from him. His dad and stepmom were the exception—I still have a great relationship with them to this day. I had gone out of my way to allow Christopher and his family to see the twins whenever it worked for them. I had bent over backwards to make everyone happy (people pleaser to my core). But on the advice of my attorney, once things had gotten contentious with the divorce, I was told not to accommodate him and his family. The rationale was that anything that would appear to be a compromise would hurt my arguments against him in court, in a few months' time. So, I followed my attorney's counsel. But after threats from Christopher that he was going to take the kids and not return them, I felt like the best thing was to protect my kids from him. He behaved unpredictably and had recently shown a dependence on drugs and a crazy lifestyle. Throughout our custody battle, Christopher said horrible things to me. He also brought up my past struggles with self-injury, depression, and anxiety to make me look like a bad mom. But the evidence that my attorney provided regarding Christopher's drug use and unstable living situation worked in my favor. The judge ordered him to take parenting classes. Christopher opposed them, until I offered to take them as well, just to prove the point that every parent has something to learn.

Christopher's mom became a thorn in my side during the divorce. When Christopher first decided to leave the marriage, she was very supportive of me. But she turned suddenly and became Christopher's biggest advocate. She financed his side of the divorce and custody proceedings. From that point on, I knew I had to handle with great caution my relationship with Christopher's mom. She will always choose her son, even over her grandchildren. I know that she loves the twins (and even me in her own way), but I also see how she has enabled her son. She loves her son beyond measure, and, as a mom, I can understand and empathize with her on that level. But I can't excuse or accept that she has chosen a relationship with her son, who is in active addiction, over a strong relationship with her grandkids who bear no responsibility in this situation.

Once the divorce was final and the custody agreement signed, Christopher had two-hour supervised visits with the twins twice a week, for which his mom had to be present at all times. After a year or so, we added an additional overnight weekend visit for him, under his mom's supervision. The first time he picked up the twins from me, I was in physical pain from the worry and the anticipated separation from the twins. I was especially alarmed knowing they were spending time with two people I did not trust at all at that point. I trusted Christopher's mom to keep the twins safe. But I didn't trust her to respect me as their mom or to not say or do things that I wouldn't necessarily agree with. Letting go of that control was hard for me. Trusting that the twins would be OK and adjust to this new normal was difficult. I felt sick to my stomach. I sat in the hallway after they picked the babies up for their first two-hour supervised visit and just sobbed for two hours—until they got back. I felt like a piece of me was missing, when they were away. It became obvious that the twins had a hard time on those first few visits. For a while, every time I walked out of the room, Lucas would cry and chase after me. The kids had learned to depend on me and me alone, up until that point. I had come to believe that my value as a person was tied to being a mom. It took me a long time to see that I had value as a person outside of my role as their mom.

On those rare Saturday nights that I had to myself, once those overnight weekend visits started about a year after our divorce was finalized, I started making plans to hang out with friends and do adult things. At local bars and nightclubs, while my friends danced, I mostly drank. I hadn't really experienced life as a single woman in the young and free stage of life, because I was either taking a double load of college classes, spending time with my nieces when they were babies, pregnant with the twins, or being a mom since I turned twenty-one. These every-other Saturday nights became my time to let loose and make some bad decisions—nothing that would put my kids in danger, since they were in their father's or grandparents' care. I would go out with friends and have a drink or two, . . . or three, or four. My girlfriends and I would have a good time talking to guys and just being single young women. After a few months of the overnight every other Saturday visits, Christopher and his mom would often cancel their visitation with the twins. It became more of a pattern as the months went on, so I learned not to make plans unless I had a backup arrangement for the twins too. Those were fun times for me as a single mom, save for the difficulties arising out of the unreliability from Christopher and his mom. But, once again, Sarah came to the rescue. She and I would hang out all the time, whether we were doing kid-friendly things with the twins or hanging out on my Saturdays as a free woman.

During this period of my life, I later realized, I had become highly codependent with Sarah. She became the other parent in the twins' lives and gave up much of her own freedom to be the best friend to me and adopted aunt to my babies. The four of us would have dance parties in the car on the way to our local playground or to an amusement park nearby. When the twins were on a visit with their father, Sarah was the one who made sure I wasn't too lonely or sad. We spent so many evenings on the porch of my apartment just talking about life, and just as many nights on the couch in that apartment watching one of the twins' favorite movies. We became a quasi-family-of-four. I knew I could count on her above anyone else and I settled into just depending on her. She will forever hold a very special place in my heart for her loyalty and devotion. I know without a doubt that the twins will always consider her a member of their family. The three of us are blessed that she chose us to love.

During this stage of life, alcohol made me bolder. Just like with my first drinking experience and then the one that landed me in the hospital shortly before I got pregnant with the twins, alcohol made me mouthy and brave. I could talk shit with the best of them and play any game a guy threw my way. I'm sure I had some bitterness toward men in general because the only man I had ever loved walked away from me without so much as a second glance. But with alcohol, I was able to be a different person, someone other than a divorcee, a mom, a hard worker, and a college graduate. I was able to be someone else, and I think at that time I didn't know who I truly was, so I was happy to put on this new mask when it was time to go out with my girls.

Just to make things a little more exciting, at a routine doctor's appointment, at around eighteen months old, Rylee was diagnosed with a heart defect known as ASD, Atrial Septal Defect. A hole in one chamber of her heart caused it to work extra hard, and it had started enlarging. The doctor wanted to schedule her surgery for that April, when she would be two and a half years old. I was scared to the core of my being. The doctor explained that they might be able to do a minimally invasive procedure through a catheter that went into an artery in Rylee's groin, up to her heart, where they would then implant a metal closure device. Since they were doing the surgery when Rylee was so young, they saw a very good prognosis for her future ability to participate in sports or activities that required a lot of endurance. After Rylee's diagnosis, I noticed, in the months prior to her surgery, that Rylee had a hard time running around with the other kids. She would get exhausted very easily, and her heart would beat out of control. It was terrifying and I started to treat her like glass. I was scared of every move she made. I was afraid of her playing too hard, of her tripping and falling. It was a very stressful time for all of us.

Rylee's heart surgeon had explained that they would not know exactly what procedure had to be done until they were able to take a picture of the back side of the hole in her heart. If the damage was not worse in the back of her heart, then they would attempt the catheter procedure instead of open-heart surgery. However, there was always a chance that they wouldn't be successful with the catheter and would have to go through with the open-heart procedure. So, when we got the test results that the heart surgeon was going to attempt the catheter procedure, I was thrilled. We had her surgery scheduled for mid-April and had all of the pre-op work taken care of. I was planning to have my dad watch Lucas during the day of the surgery, and I would spend my day and night (and possibly a few days and nights depending on her recovery rate) in the hospital by Rylee's side. I hated having to deal with Christopher during this process. Though he tried acting like the doting father, he often failed to attend doctor's visits, because, his mom suggested, he felt too overwhelmed. She said that he coped badly with anxiety. But I had a tough time feeling sorry for him. So, I focused on Rylee. I scheduled as many fun things as possible in the weeks before her surgery, since she would be on watch for a few weeks following the procedure. I explained the process to her as simply as I could, so that she wasn't terrified when we showed up at the hospital.

Rylee has always been smart. Too smart for her own good sometimes when she was little, and sneaky to boot. If you ever meet Sarah, ask her how many times Rylee got away with finding scissors and playing hairdresser on her own hair, on Sarah's watch. It was a running joke for a while that Rylee would for sure be a hairstylist when she grew up, and she was getting her practice hours in early. Some great photos of her between the ages of four and six show her with bangs chopped sideways or chunks of her hair missing on the side of her face.

Rylee was a very bright two-year-old and she understood that her heart was broken and she had to go to the hospital to have it fixed. But I reassured her that mommy would be there every step of the way, and that seemed to comfort her. The night before her surgery, I didn't sleep at all. I stayed awake and watched my daughter sleep in my bed next to me. I had wrestled with religion and faith in the past, but, that night I just prayed and cried. I pleaded with God to let her make it through all of these trials. I promised to be a better person and a better mom if He would just fix her heart. In those moments of waiting and praying, I knew that there was a God who was listening and heard my prayers. I knew that there had to be a God who had looked out for the twins in the NICU and who had pushed Lucas to take those first few breaths. The prospect of the operation scared me to death. But I had to trust that God would be looking out for my baby girl. However, first, we had to get through the worst of it.

As a girl raised in a conservative Christian home, when I faced difficulties, I would hear my dad suggest getting more involved at church, praying, and generally being "churched up" to fix my problems. He had become a Christian as an adult, and, to this day, depends heavily on his faith and the routines he has created around his belief. I've always admired that about him, even if I have struggled with my own faith over the years. Especially after going to a Christian high school and seeing the hypocrisy in some of the school leaders' decisions regarding girls who got pregnant as juniors or seniors. I found it disgusting that they chose to expel the girls, but allowed the boy who had gotten one of the girls pregnant to remain at school. I think it was around this time that I started to turn away from church and religion. I've wavered on my faith over the years. I too often failed to heed my dad's encouragement to look to God in moments of desperation, when at my lowest and most vulnerable. But at times, when in a situation I have felt is out of my control, the draw to a God that looks out for those who need it most has become irresistible. Faced with the possibility of losing my baby girl, more than ever I relied on the hope that God would lend a hand and keep innocent Rylee alive.

Watching Rylee be put under anesthesia was one of the most difficult things to endure. It was gut-wrenching to see my spunky kid suddenly motionless. But we made it through that part, and when the surgeon came out and said all went perfectly, I felt the relief course through my body. In the recovery room, I saw my baby girl with a splint on her leg, to keep her from moving and disturbing the artery that had been used for the catheter that carried the metal closure device to her heart. Her eyes and mouth were slightly open, but it was clear that she was in a deep sleep. When she started mumbling, I jumped up to her side. She whispered, "Mama. . . .," still half asleep, and tears filled my eyes. I knew when I heard her voice that she would be OK. She was on the road to recovery and, in that moment, I sent a million thanks up to God for keeping a watchful eye on my little girl.

Immediately after her surgery, Rylee was required to take it easy for a few days. We then went back and had the heart surgeon check her out. He gave her clearance to do normal activities for the following six months, though nothing that could cause a sudden jolt to her heart (no bounce houses, no trampolines, etc.). She was re-checked for a six months' post-op and was given the full go-ahead to pursue activities of her choosing and to come back for a repeat EKG and echocardiogram every two years.

Christopher showed up to the hospital, though late, the day Rylee had her surgery. He had his mom with him, and they both stayed in the waiting area during Rylee's surgery. Christopher was too tired to stick around for very long after Rylee woke up. I think he saw her for a minute or two before taking off. He left it up to me to stand by her, as he has for the last decade.

Rylee is turning eighteen this year. She has no remaining complications from her heart condition. She's a fighter, always has been, and I have every reason to believe that she always will be. Whenever I think about how brave and tough she is, how much smarter she is than I was at her age when it comes to making good choices for herself, I'm amazed by her feisty spirit and her strong will. These traits have made it a little more challenging to raise her, but I hope they continue defining her. I could not be more proud of the young woman that she's turning into. If I hold any resentment toward Christopher for his lack of involvement in her life, it's quickly replaced by a feeling of pity for him that he doesn't know his daughter—nor his son. He is missing out.

Chapter 10

Mark

In the months leading up to Rylee's heart surgery, I was in the midst of my "party girl every other Saturday night" phase. I was spending a lot of time with an old friend of mine who had relocated to Southern California after living in Las Vegas for a few years. A break-up with her boyfriend in Vegas precipitated her return home. Kenzie* and I had grown up playing soccer together. She was my fun friend, and we would hang out a lot on the Saturdays when I didn't have my kids. She would also spend time with the kids and me most weekends. Kenzie was always an easy person to get along with, and I enjoyed her carefree attitude about life. Shortly after her move back to California, she became interested in this guy we used to know in high school, Jeff.* I had a lot of fun with the two of them, even when I was the third wheel. They became two of my closest friends. Jeff also had a military buddy who started to come along with them. Mark* did not strike me as terribly bright, but, every now and then, I saw sparks of kindness and substance to him. Mark and I built this unhealthy "non-relationship"—no strings attached between us—over the next few months. I'm pretty sure he was having similar non-relationships with other girls from work and who knows where else. I just wanted to keep my interactions with

---

* Some names in this story have been changed for privacy reasons.

him clean and easy. This involvement with Mark began at a Halloween party at my sister's house in 2008. I invited Kenzie and Jeff, and they brought Mark along for the ride. Toward the end of the night, Kenzie had wandered off with Jeff to have sex in the back of his car. Mark and I were talking in front of the house, and, in a blur of too many shots and mixed drinks, Mark seemed like a decent enough guy to me. He kissed me and we made tentative plans to hang out in the near future . . . When it was convenient . . . If we both wanted to. Very tentative. No commitment.

The only thing about him that mattered to me was our physical non-relationship. So, I wanted to keep Mark separate from everything else in my life that mattered. Over the next couple of months, Mark and I hung out with Kenzie and Jeff a few times, making out in movie theaters or at Jeff's house, and then taking things to the next level in a hotel room in San Diego. Kenzie and I had taken a weekend girls' trip, and Jeff and Mark decided to come down for the night since Mark's family lived nearby. Mark was the second man I had sex with, as Christopher was the only one I had slept with before that night. When I had hooked up with random guys at bars, it never went past kissing. Physical intimacy scared me, so I had kept it very PG—up until that point. I let my guard down with Mark. I rationalized that he was different. I told myself that he was "safe," because he was friends with people I loved and trusted. It was an altogether weird experience. I liked hanging out with Mark, but only as long as there was alcohol involved. Sober, I didn't find anything very appealing about him. Perhaps, Mark was a distraction that would help me work through the pain caused by the failure of my marriage. I don't know what Mark thought I was going to be to him. I do know that I reminded him on multiple occasions that I in no way wanted or expected a relationship from him. I wanted to have a purely physical connection when we hung out. I wanted to hang out only when it was convenient for both of us.

Mark and I had been hanging out for a few months, when Jeff's father passed away unexpectedly. All four of us took a road trip to

Nevada to attend the funeral. It was the first time I'd been gone for the weekend since I became a mom. I had left my kids with my parents for two nights, so that I could go to the funeral and support Jeff and Kenzie. At that point, Kenzie and I had gotten very close, and I wanted to be emotionally and physically present for her. Jeff and Kenzie stayed with Jeff's brother, and Mark and I stayed in a hotel. Mark drank way too much, and started acting like a possessive boyfriend everywhere we went. In the hotel, he would grab at me and get jealous if I talked to any other guy—even to a waiter trying to take my drink order. Mark's behavior began freaking me out. Then, the night after the funeral, we were walking from the car to the hotel room when Mark started crying and telling me how much I meant to him and how he felt like nothing else he did in his life was good. He didn't have a solid career, even though he'd been volunteering at the fire department for three years and had finished his fire academy training. He confided that he wasn't close to his family. He also felt like his friendship with Jeff was slipping away, because Jeff was getting so close to Kenzie since his father's passing.

Mark was sobbing by the time we got to the hotel room. I just wanted to get him inside the room and make him shut up. I felt embarrassed by his loud public display of emotion. But he was tugging at my heart strings and I felt for him—which was exactly what I didn't want, going into this whole thing. He was supposed to be my fun, non-relationship guy. We weren't supposed to have actual conversations and get to know each other on a deep level. I felt stuck. I started to panic. I asked him to go get some ice for me just to get him out of the room for a little bit. Instead, he started undressing and yelling at me to help him. Mark pushed me toward the bed and I landed on the mattress. I was sitting on the edge of the bed as he kept screaming at me, tears coming down his cheeks. If he meant anything to me, he wanted me to show it, he shouted. I was so stunned by his outburst that I was frozen on the bed. I couldn't move. Mark carried on with his rant for a few more minutes, until he saw the look on my face and it finally seemed to sink in that he was scaring me. He reached out to touch my cheek, and I snapped my head to the side, as if he might actually hit me.

Mark started apologizing and telling me he never meant to scare me, and asked what he could do to make it better. He was still drunk, and he wanted to make things better, so I had sex with him to appease him and in an attempt to calm my own fears. It was a miserable night, and I was worried, felt bewildered, and did not know what to do or what, if anything, I would be able to do. I knew something had to change with Mark, and I knew nothing would ever be the same again after that night because the sudden fear of him had so jolted me. The trip home was quiet. When we got back to California, I cut back on my contact with Mark and would rarely text him. But I found out that Jeff, Kenzie, and Mark were planning to move in together in just a few short weeks.

This prospect made me feel even more trapped. What could I do? Mark's birthday was coming up, and I knew that Kenzie expected me to attend the celebration. Following his birthday party, Mark and I ended up spending the night together. A couple of months later was Jeff's birthday—and I again wound up spending the night with Mark. Feeling like I might have gotten myself in a situation that I couldn't get out of, I suddenly wondered whether I didn't want to get out of it. About a month later, Mark started hinting at us being more than just "friends" and wanting to be in a relationship with me. I freaked out and reminded him that I had never set out to be in a relationship with him and that I had been clear about it. But I told Mark that I did want him to be at my birthday party the following weekend. He agreed to come. He also said that he wasn't going to be happy with our arrangement for too much longer.

For my twenty-seventh birthday, my sister and closest friends had planned a party for me at my sister's house. I had a blast, with a ton of my old friends showing up to celebrate, including a newly pregnant Kenzie, and my kindergarten bestie, Natalie. Sarah and

Laura were there too, because that's what those two have always done for me—shown up unfailingly. I steered clear of Mark until the point where I could explain everything away with alcohol. When a friend of mine started talking to Mark, I got really jealous and made sure to put a stop to that conversation pronto. When Mark started acting angry and quiet, I poked at him and then flirted with any other guy who was around. I behaved like a total bitch to him.

Mark and I left the party around midnight. I was fully intoxicated—but my kids were tucked away safely at my parents' house. I don't remember all of the details of that night. I do remember walking up to my apartment door, Mark next to me. I also remember him pushing me onto the bed and pulling my jeans off. The next thing I remember is waking up on the cold, hard bathroom floor, fully naked under a towel I was wrapped in, feeling like I had been hit by a bus. I had bruises forming on my inner thighs and my shoulders. I had fingerprint bruises up and down my arms, and along the sides of my rib cage. I was shocked by what I saw.

Mark was nowhere to be found. I texted him and asked what had happened the night before. When I got his curt response, "I had a good time. . . . You deserved it. . . . ," I felt like I couldn't breathe. The reality of what had happened to me started seeping in. I began feeling anguished and vulnerable. I called Kenzie for support, but all she said was, "Well you probably asked for it." I felt a jab of pain hearing my best friend say something like that and show no sympathy toward me. I had just been brutalized by Mark—someone who claimed to care about me, and all my best friend could say was that I'd asked for it? In that moment, I knew that no matter what happened between Kenzie and me moving forward, our friendship would never be the same again. After that day, I didn't talk to Mark again. We went our separate ways and I found out the following weekend, when I was celebrating my birthday with a few friends, that they had spotted him out on a date with another girl. He had known about my birthday plans with my friends that weekend and

I was disappointed that he hadn't even so much as sent me a happy birthday text. In spite of the assault I had experienced at Mark's hands, I was still in a muddled state and I still felt connected to him and had some fondness for him.

A few days after my birthday, Sarah, my sister, and my brother-in-law all pulled me aside to tell me I needed to slow down with my drinking. They could tell I was dangerously intoxicated when I left my birthday party with Mark. They had all tried to stop me but I was adamant that I was fine and in control. I didn't remember any of these conversations. This was one of the first times that I was called out on my drinking behavior, and it was coming from three of the people I trusted most at that point in my life. When I look back and think about the opportunities along the way that could have caused me to get sober many years before, I think that I wasn't ready to recognize the way that alcohol took over my willpower, my deepest identity. It made me into a different person, because it took down all of the people pleasing, perfectionist tendencies that my sober self was devoted to. It stripped me of my inhibitions and made the pain less hurtful, at least temporarily.

Chapter 11

New Beginnings

Around my birthday in 2009, I started talking to a guy that I really liked. This was before the days of Tinder and Bumble. It just wasn't going anywhere when I had tried meeting people out in clubs (not the best spot to meet your husband as Ed Sheeran argues). I had gone on a few boring dinner and movie dates, but nothing really stuck. I tried online dating through eharmony. A few guys I met were marginally more fun to hang out with and I dated them casually for a couple of weeks at most. I didn't drink on any of these dates. I was the best version of myself, hoping that something real would develop. Perhaps then I could find the person in my life whom I was ready for. This man I could get serious about. I would be able to stop trying to fill the void with alcohol or with a . . . messy-from-the-start non-relationship.

This guy I was talking to online through eharmony was ready to meet in person. Nick had shared beautiful stories with me via email. We had talked on the phone and texted. I had been exploring new things since I had become single. Adventures in the wild were something new that had piqued my interest—I had not been into nature beforehand. I shared with him that I was going on a trip to Yosemite with Sarah and a friend from out of town who was visiting her for the summer. Nick seemed very interested in hearing about this impending trip. It was one of the things we connected on. I'm grateful for the timing of that trip, because it appeared to create this instant bond for Nick and me to build on. My interactions with him made him seem like a genuinely good man, an authentic person, and a safe place to land.

The first time I met Nick in person, we had a couple of drinks at a local restaurant. With him, things were comfortable and conversation was easy from the start. Because of that, I became terrified that he might want nothing to do with me on a physical level. Nick and I hung out several times with no more than a hug exchanged. We got to know each other really well, asking all of the questions that come naturally as you get to know someone. But I had experienced giving priority to the physical part of a relationship with Mark. So, I felt like Nick may not be finding me attractive, because he wasn't rushing into getting physical with me. He seemed to genuinely care about what I thought, what I liked, and what I dreamed of doing in the future. He wanted to hear me talk and find out as much as he could about me. Nick shared that he had been in a very serious relationship that was toxic. It appeared to be as destructive as my relationship with Christopher had been. Nick knew what it felt like to be betrayed by someone you love. Just when I had given up on finding a guy that was worthy of my and my kids' time, I found someone who fit very smoothly into my life from the beginning. I never felt any pressure from him to be something that I'm not and we seemed to instantly click. Now, it was not love at first sight. In hindsight, I had to admit that it was a good thing. It meant we had a chance to be real and our bond could be solid—and was not built on first impressions or superficial notions.

Nick was great with the twins from the very beginning as well. I think I introduced him to them after we'd been seriously hanging out for about a month. They were almost three years old at that point. He was never pushy, never forced them to accept or love him before they were ready. He was a stable presence in their lives, and provided support and love without being aggressive about what his role needed to be in their lives. So, he showed up for my kids, just like he has always shown up for me. That night at my apartment, Nick and I finally shared our first kiss. It was the type of kiss that makes you want to know more about a person. Kissing him made me want to kiss him more, and it made me want to know him and spend more time with him. It felt right to be in his arms. I wanted to see where this was headed. We took our time moving from the first kiss to the more intimate stages of our physical relationship. But that first kiss made me see all of the things about Nick that I needed in my life: his grounding nature, his calmness, his logical perspective on everything. The latter trait balanced out my emotional approach and the way I tended to negotiate the pieces of my life that were still a bit messy (like sharing custody of the twins). And it gave me hope for a future with someone who would embrace everything about me, and maybe even love me one day.

A few months after meeting, Nick and I went on a trip to attend his cousin's wedding in a little town in Northern California. The eight-hour car ride gave us more time to get to know each other. When I left a day early to get back in time for my mom's birthday, saying goodbye to Nick and the flight home from Sacramento were a lot tougher than I had thought they would be. I knew then that I was falling hard for this guy. I knew that I wanted to spend more and more time with him. Nick started staying the night at my apartment a couple of days a week, and at least one weekend night. The twins got to know him, and we would do lots of fun stuff as a group of four. We took the kids to Knott's Berry Farm, we went out to dinner with them, spent time at the playground with them, and watched movies at home while eating popcorn and ice cream.

Nick fit seamlessly into our lives. If I had a bad day, felt burnt out and exhausted by single motherhood, I had a welcoming shoulder to cry on and a man who cared about me and what I was going through. My family and friends accepted Nick from the beginning. I felt like part of his family too. New Year's Eve 2009 with Nick was the best I have ever had, hands-down. We exchanged a beautiful New Year's

Eve kiss full of passion and love and commitment. Neither one of us had been willing to express feelings of attachment quite yet. But I knew in my heart and in my head that I had fallen completely in love with him. I also knew I wasn't going to be the first one to reveal how I felt. I hoped that he was close to whispering those words. But I would grow accustomed to the way that he wanted to make sure the timing was perfect. For the time being, I knew he wanted to be in my life. I knew that he wanted to be in the twins' lives, if that meant being a part of my life. After those first holidays together, Halloween, Thanksgiving, Christmas, and then New Year's Eve, we spent New Year's Day in the snow with the twins—their first time ever in the snow! Like so many of our experiences with Nick, it wasn't a perfect day (there were tears and meltdowns about wet socks and being cold and hungry), but it was real and it was fun. It bonded the four of us in shared experiences together. It was one of those moments that solidified the relationship Nick and I were building, and it made me wonderfully happy and grateful.

I finally heard those three little words from Nick a week before Valentine's Day. Holding me tight, he was so sweet as he whispered them in my ear. I melted into his arms, and from that moment on, we became inseparable. That spring, we spent a lot of time together and then moved in together. The presence of alcohol was minimal at most. We would have a drink here or there if we went out to eat. But there wasn't an excessive amount of drinking in that first year we spent as a couple. Nick wasn't a big drinker. He'd occasionally have a whiskey on ice or a few beers at a party or gathering, but that was it. He didn't appear to have a troubling relationship with alcohol from my perspective.

A few weeks after Nick and I celebrated our one-year dating anniversary that following summer, I realized that my period was several days late. I had been on birth control since a few weeks after the twins were born. I could feel that something was off within a couple of days of my missed period. I shared what was happening with Nick about a week after I first noticed it, along with my concern.

Nick took the news as well as any man could. He was excited about adding to our family, even if it wasn't the most ideal timing, since we hadn't been planning on having a child anytime soon, after a mere year together. He was so reassuring, supportive, loving, and kind that I couldn't help but get excited too. I was looking forward to co-parenting with a man who wanted to be involved and to share in those experiences with me. I took a pregnancy test, and sure enough, the faint line popped up. I was pregnant. I knew I couldn't be more than about four or five weeks pregnant. I was worried about things going wrong, since I had suffered through a miscarriage before getting pregnant with the twins. I was also nervous about what people would think, because Nick and I were not married. The only thing that should have mattered was what Nick and I thought, and how Lucas and Rylee would react to the news. But the opinion of others was still a concern for the people-pleaser in me.

Two days after my positive pregnancy test, the morning that I was planning to call and make a doctor's appointment, I started bleeding and experiencing intense abdominal cramping. I recognized the signs and fell apart. I felt wretched sadness at the loss of this child, one created in love and one that I had already started to fall in love with. I called Nick and told him the news. He shared his sadness with me. He was also supportive of me and my pain, and wanted to do nothing more than to hold me and make me feel better. Losing a child is not only physically painful. It tears you up emotionally. It is one of the toughest experiences I have ever gone through, and it doesn't get any easier the second time around. I called my doctor to make sure I was handling the situation as responsibly as possible. She said that, since I couldn't have been more than five weeks pregnant, what I had experienced was what they called a chemical pregnancy. My body was pregnant, but because it was in early stages, no procedure was needed at this juncture. But this time, I had support all around me and I didn't have to resort to self-destructive behaviors, like I had in the past, to cope with this devastating development. I felt grounded for the first time in a long time.

About six months after we moved in together, Nick proposed. It was a beautiful night. Summer was on its way out in Southern California, and there was a crisp breeze in the air. Nick took me to a beautiful hilltop restaurant, and holding me close while we looked out over the city lights, he whispered in my ear that I was the best thing that had ever happened to him, and that he wanted to spend the rest of his life with me. He asked me to be his wife, and I said yes. We discussed having our wedding in December of that year. We thus had a little over three months to make arrangements and only a couple weeks to get the invitations out. But we knew what we wanted, and we wanted each other forever. So why postpone the inevitable?

Wedding planning began a few days—actually a few hours—after our engagement. Nick and I both knew that we didn't want a huge wedding. So, we decided on a simple wedding in Las Vegas, in one of the nice hotel chapels that could accommodate our friends and family. We could have a wedding without spending tens of thousands of dollars on one day in our lives. We picked out simple flowers. I shopped for my wedding gown and bridesmaid dresses. I helped Nick pick out groomsmen tuxedoes. The entire wedding party was going to wear black Converse instead of fancy shoes. One of my favorite parts of the wedding was seeing Lucas, Rylee, my nieces and our new nephew in tiny little black Converse. So cute!

Nick and I never drank a ton together at the beginning of our relationship. We would each have a drink or two. If one of us was drinking a lot, the other one would stay sober. Usually, I would be the one drinking more. It was on rare occasions that Nick drank more than he should have, in those early years of dating and marriage. Alcohol wasn't a big part of our dating story at all. I don't recall any times in those early years where things got very sloppy on my end. I usually kept it together and would just have a slight hangover the next day.

Things changed a year or two after we got married. I was feeling unfulfilled with my career. I started drinking unhealthy amounts of alcohol on a regular basis. Pretty much every night after work, I drank excessively. I gained weight and started to really hate myself. It became a vicious cycle: the more weight I put on, the more I hated myself, the more I tried to numb my feelings with alcohol. Nick worked a lot when we were first married, so, in a lot of ways, I still felt like a single parent sometimes. He was also going back to school during the first couple of years of our marriage. I could not repress feelings of jealousy that he was pursuing some of his dreams while I was stuck at a job I hated. I needed to tackle in a responsible way what were my own issues. But, instead, I tried to hide in a bottle of whiskey.

Looking at photos taken at my thirtieth birthday party at the house we were renting, I am reminded of what pretty much everyone bought me for my birthday that year: giant bottles of Jack Daniels. These were all gone within a couple of weeks. Alcohol had definitely shown backup as a serious problem in my life, but I wasn't ready to face it.

Chapter 12

Friendships

Before I met Nick, I had a couple of very close friends in my life and I did everything with them. One of those friends was Sarah. Another, Callie*, was part of a friend group connected to my sister. I started socializing with her and she and I got close. She loved to go out and drink and have adventures. Her husband didn't mind when she went out with the girls and let loose. Callie was exactly the right friend for me at that time in my life. Sarah, Callie, and I were like the three amigos for a solid year or two before I married Nick. The year I got married, Callie's mom passed away at a very young age from cancer. Callie found out she was pregnant around the same time, after trying to conceive for a few years. We were there for each other in a lot of ways. Even though we are not close anymore, I'll always be grateful for the friendship we shared during that time of our lives.

Two years after Nick and I got married, Callie asked me to go with her to New York City. The trip was meant to honor and remember her mom, because the city was one of her favorite places. Earlier that same year, the friend from out of town who had gone with Sarah and me to Yosemite, Heather*, asked me to meet her in Chicago for a girls' trip. I jumped at both chances to escape my real life. I had

---

* Some names in this story have been changed for privacy reasons.

started to resent Nick for what had become too tame and boring an existence for me. I felt entitled to this resentment because he was the one who had helped create this normal, calm, steady life with me. I went to both Chicago and New York City. I found emotional intimacy and closeness with my friends rather than with my husband. At the time, I often treated the friends in my life as more of a priority than Nick. Even though he was exactly what I needed, which I knew from the get-go, I believe that I felt like I didn't deserve him or the steadiness that he provided. I didn't treat him well. It took me almost thirteen years to recognize that and apologize to him wholeheartedly for not appreciating him during those early years of our marriage.

Both trips with Callie and Heather included drinking, and one night in Chicago is particularly hazy. I drank far more out in public than I ever had in the past, and some of the details of that night are still unclear. Heather swears that our drinks were roofied. I vaguely recall talking to a couple of guys in a bar down the street from our hotel. I have a memory of peeing on the street on the way back to our hotel—not a moment I'm proud of. I recall waking up in our hotel room with the worst headache at around five in the morning. These trips were another way to hide from the things I disliked so much about myself. They were an attempt to avoid dealing with the issues in my marriage that I'd been running from. Just as alcohol had been for me for over fifteen years at that point, they were another escape mechanism.

I am working toward holding myself accountable, in my newfound sobriety. It took me way too long to face how the way I conducted myself damaged me and others around me. Clarity has come to me with my sobriety and there's no turning back now. I want to focus on owning my mistakes, and move forward in a healthy way with the people who are meant to be a part of my life.

We all know that change is never easy. Changing a behavior that one has used to cope for many years is particularly difficult.

I've had to walk away from a few different destructive coping mechanisms in my life, including self-injury, an eating disorder, and an unhealthy relationship with alcohol. What came next was the need to do the work to choose a different path and to write my own story. According to Karolina Rzadkowolska in her book *Euphoric: Ditch Alcohol and Gain a Happier, More Confident You,* "Getting out of your comfort zone is hard, and drinking happens to be an ultimate comfort zone behavior. The part of you that doesn't want to change will scream at you with excuses and limiting stories about what this means for your life. But I know you've done hard things before and felt wildly fulfilled afterward. And I know you've also taken it easy and felt stuck and regretful."[7] Although the journey (one I've attempted many times in the past with little success) has been difficult, I'm incredibly grateful for the chance to start again and write my own narrative, based on what I've been through and intending on not letting that define where I'm going.

---

7   Karolina Rzadkowolska. *Euphoric: Ditch Alcohol and Gain a Happier, More Confident You,* HarperCollins Focus LLC, 2022, 13.

Jenn Burton

Chapter 13

Going Through the Motions

In 2012, less than two years after Nick and I had been married and when the twins were in kindergarten, I hit a wall. I was working at a local school district in the human resources department. I had made my first attempt at a career change earlier that year, going so far as to complete four courses and pass a couple of entrance exams to begin a teacher credential program. My goal was to become a high school teacher, and then go on to teach community college classes. Meanwhile, I applied to an adjunct professor position at the university I had attended for my undergraduate and graduate degrees. My application and sample syllabus were accepted, and I was assigned to teach a course titled "Women in American Society" that upcoming fall semester. I was beyond excited—and terrified. To accommodate the course's schedule, I needed permission to leave work one hour early one day a week. My supervisor said the department would not be able to accommodate that schedule change. I had to be in the office until four thirty every day, to field questions from visitors, job applicants, or employees. I was devastated. I had already put energy into creating a perfect syllabus. I so looked forward to this next step in my career. But my dreams now seemed to be crumbling. When I turned down the adjunct professor job, I felt deep grief.

When I had to let go of that opportunity, my dream of becoming a college professor appeared to be dead. At that point, I seemed to begin just going through the motions in my life. I know that it affected my relationship with my husband and my relationship with my kids. I started drinking every night, stopping on my lunch break to pick up another bottle. I might have convinced myself that morning that I was breaking the nightly drinking cycle, but I kept getting that next bottle. Every day, after work, I would pick up my kids from daycare. On the way back home, I would stop at a fast-food place. I would order dinner for them. For me, I would ask for an extra-large diet soda. I would mix the soda with whiskey, as soon as I walked in the door at home. It was a cycle I couldn't break out of. I wasn't processing the profound disappointment of the missed opportunity and was instead drowning my sorrows in alcohol. I pretended it was all OK. I told myself that I had to focus on the job I still had and the kids I was raising. I should try not to let my new marriage fall apart.

In reality, I was cheating everyone around me out of having an actual relationship with me: all I cared about was when I would be able to drink all my emotions away. My thoughts were consumed with when I would be able to drink next. Then, I would go to work pretty much every day with a hangover. I then would start all over again by five that evening. I would fall asleep, or black out, on the couch many nights. I would stumble to my bed, only to repeat the cycle day after day.

Less than two years into a new marriage, I had twins in kindergarten. I felt stuck in a job that I started to resent because I couldn't pursue my dream of becoming a college professor—which had appeared well within my grasp. So, I was in a very dark place in 2012. I was reminded that my relationship with alcohol was unhealthy. Drinking had become my go-to choice for numbing the pain caused by the discontent in my everyday life.

One day, I made the decision to reach out to my oldest and dearest friend, my kindergarten bestie and protector, Natalie. She invited me to an AA meeting. I felt like that meeting would provide a chance for me to embrace the fact that I had an unhealthy relationship with alcohol. But I immediately faced obstacles. I didn't like having to say that I was powerless over alcohol, as the AA process required all attendees to admit. AA also had participants introduce themselves by declaring "I am an alcoholic." I was shocked by the prospect of having to live with such a label for the rest of my life. Admitting to having an unhealthy relationship with alcohol is not the same as acknowledging having an addiction. Somewhere inside me, I seemed to hold on to the conviction that I could just moderate my drinking. I could make some changes and everything would work out. So, I did not dive head first into AA that night. But that meeting had put the organization and its approach on my radar. It also awakened me to the possibility that there might be other solutions that could help with what I was going through and with what I needed in order to deal with an issue that kept resurfacing.

In the online sober communities, like Lighthouse Sobriety and The Sober Mom Life Cafe, that I now attend, we talk about the mental gymnastics of this cycle. We discuss how the thought of drinking, and planning out when and how many, and moderating our consumption just consumes every inch of your brain power. We share about the physical and emotional dependency on that dopamine hit. The drinks after the first one don't really deliver any more dopamine. Thereafter, you're just chasing that same initial feeling. After educating myself on the effects of alcohol, I found out about the toxins it contains and what it does to your brain, your body, and your sleep. It seems incredible to me how the culture we live in pushes alcohol at women, and especially moms, at every turn. From social media images of "mommy wine culture" and needing alcohol to survive motherhood, to summertime décor at the local home goods store screaming that "it's beer-thirty" and "wine o'clock" all day long when the sun is shining, we are bombarded with such messages. We believe that we need wine to survive our children. We buy into the notion that we deserve a beer after a hard day of juggling work, home, and the kids. If we don't drink, we're the ones who have a problem. The message to drink poison in order to stay happy and able to do all we are responsible for seems to be mind-blowingly effective.

Chapter 14

My Anchor Baby & New Chapters

In early 2013, I was having a lot of trouble with my ankle, which I had broken in high school. I was having severe tendon pain in my foot. A podiatrist I had a consultation with recommended surgery to repair damage to the tendon that had developed during post-injury recovery. I had been gradually gaining weight since my wedding. I was now over two hundred thirty pounds and wholly uncomfortable with and in my body. Nick had expressed concern about the amount of alcohol I was drinking on a regular basis. As a result, he and I were having some rancorous fights. With work aspirations being disappointed, my unfulfilling income-earning job, intense physical pain from my foot, and my weight struggles, it seemed most aspects in my life were a disaster. I had help from my parents with the twins, now in kindergarten, after school and on days off. Chaos was reigning in my head and drinking was all-consuming at that point. But the twins were living a normal life, thanks to the network of people around us who loved them and kept things stable. Their biological dad had dropped almost completely out of the picture by this time. He saw them a few times a year. His own addiction and self-destruction had led him down a path that made it unsafe for the twins to be around him without someone else involved (usually their paternal grandmother). His addiction also prevented him from making the twins a priority. During that time, thankfully, the twins had my parents, Auntie Sarah, and my sister and her husband in their lives. They were the constants that the twins had come to depend on. They could observe and sense how compromised the stability of their own mom was, whether they knew how to express that at the time.

After I had my foot surgery in the spring of 2013, I was out of work for a couple of months on disability. I took advantage of that time off to cut back on drinking and do some creative projects to keep my mind busy while my body was healing. I did cut back on drinking and I completed two scrapbooks for the twins. I had created baby scrapbooks for them up to age one. I thoroughly enjoyed completing scrapbooks for the next stage of their life. I have always appreciated creative outlets, like painting (not well), doing puzzles, writing, or making scrapbooks. So, this down time was the perfect occasion for getting to a healthier place. About a month into my recovery from surgery, I started to feel the tell-tale signs that I might be pregnant again. Nick and I had agreed that we were ready to have a baby together, despite the difficulties in our marriage at the time. We had discussed early on our desire to add to our family and have one child together, and the timing seemed appropriate. So, I had gone off birth control sometime in the last year.

In May 2013, I confirmed that I was pregnant. Still on disability leave from work, I had another month or so before I needed to return to my job. I prayed for this baby to make it to term and be born healthy and without issues. I was scared that this birth might be as stressful and frightening as the birth of the first of the twins, Lucas. I was anxious for most of that pregnancy. In the summer of 2013, we found out that we were having a baby boy. We pretty quickly decided on the name Micah Daniel. Daniel was chosen in remembrance of Nick's older brother, who had passed away tragically in an accident the year the twins were born, before I met Nick. Micah just felt right. It was a strong name, and I hoped that this solid name would reflect the baby's resilience. My pregnancy was a little bit tougher this time. I had infection after infection, resulting in the need for antibiotics and then I would experience reactions to the antibiotics. My son is allergic to penicillin, and I cannot help but wonder if that may be a reaction from him to too many antibiotics in utero. The anxiety during this pregnancy had me worried about everything. And to top it off, Nick and I had decided to make a move about an hour away from where we were living in Orange County, California. My parents, my sister and her family, and our closest friends all lived within a fifteen-minute radius of one another. Because we wanted to buy a house, we had to move at least an hour away to be able to afford the type of residence we wanted for our growing family. We started looking at houses when I was four months pregnant, and put an offer on a house almost two months later. I felt like I was disappointing my family by moving the twins, and now this new baby, so far away from them. The stress from that sense of letting my loved ones down was difficult for me to manage. But I knew I wanted my kids to have a stable home life and a place that would always be a home base for them and that just wasn't possible in OC.

One of the best things about pregnancy was how easy it was for me not to drink. I never questioned sobriety during pregnancy. It was just a given. I had no cravings, no need to drown out my feelings. I was hyper-focused on my baby and wanting a fresh start with my husband. My pregnancy with Micah was one of the best things that happened to us as a family. But in the ninth month, I suffered from severe anxiety. The holidays were upon us and with them came the expected extra pressures. I wanted to make sure the twins had a great Christmas. It was also a lot to juggle to organize their visits with their dad's side of the family, and incorporating Nick's family into the plans as well. I had never been through the last month of pregnancy, since the twins were almost six weeks early. These final four weeks were utterly uncomfortable physically. I was miserable from feeling constant strain in my hips and lower back. I wanted Micah to join us out in the world as soon as it was healthy for him to do so. Sometime in mid-December, I thought that I was in labor and went to the hospital. But it was a false alarm.

Toward the end of December, I went in for one of my last regular prenatal checkup appointments and pleaded with the doctor to induce me a week early. I was in a lot of pain and was ready for the baby to be born. Micah had plans of his own, of course. His due date was January 7, 2014. On January 3, my doctor agreed to schedule me for a C-section the coming Sunday, January 5, 2014. That morning, I woke up, riddled with anxiety and completely stressed out. I wanted to meet my baby boy, but I was so fearful that something would go wrong with the birth that having a C-section felt like the right decision. He would be born seconds after they cut me open and they could make sure he was healthy. There would be none of the worry that might come from waiting hours while I would be trying to push him out. The doctor also said that he expected it to be a big baby, and there may be issues with his being born naturally. So, all-in-all, the C-section was the right way to go for me at the time. I don't regret that decision one bit.

Micah Daniel was born on January 5, 2014, at a whopping eight pounds twelve ounces. He was handsome and serious from the moment he was born. His little face was perfect. He was perfect. I was in a lot of pain after that C-section. It was a much different experience than the one I had had with the twins. Nick was a supportive partner through all of this. Poor guy. . . . I was extraordinarily difficult to deal with during that last month. I even left him at a restaurant one day, because he made me mad (possibly for as stupid a reason as forgetting to order extra cheese on my tacos). My sister had to go pick him up. When I think about the ways that I treated him in the past, I feel a great sense of shame. He's a good man, and I'm grateful that he'll pass down some of his traits to our boys. A little over a year later, Micah welcomed his baby brother, Jaxon. Each of my sons carries traits of their dad that I am so glad they share with him. Micah, being Nick's first biological child, has a lot in common with his dad, but he also has my emotional side, my sensitivity, my overly analytical tendencies. There is no doubt that Micah is an HSP, just like his mom. Parenting an HSP has given me a newfound respect for my parents and what they dealt with when I was a child. I hope that I can help guide Micah through life as someone who feels things more deeply than others around him. He's not just sensitive and wildly smart, he's also sarcastic and witty. He is one of my favorite humans. Even if he weren't my kid, I'd want to hang out with him. He's all the best pieces of Nick and me wrapped up in one. From the beginning, I called him my anchor baby, because he anchored me to reality. Micah grounds me in a way that no one else does. He is also always checking in on how I'm feeling. We have that HSP vibe going strong between us, and I feel lucky to be his mom.

Once we moved to our new home outside of Orange County, a lot of important memories were created for the twins. This move for our new family of five was one of the best decisions Nick and I ever made. Our relationship was getting a lot better. I was not seeing much of most of my friends. With a new baby, I was less willing to stay out late or do things that would affect our sleep schedules. Still plagued with anxiety when Micah was a baby, I didn't leave him for more than a few minutes at a time. We co-slept, Micah sharing our bed for the first few years of his life. I worked from home and Micah was my sidekick everywhere I went. We had a very close bond. I felt like I had a renewed sense of purpose in being his mom. I loved watching Nick become a biological dad. He clearly loved Micah and was very protective of him. He also trusted me as a caregiver—he told me regularly that I was a good mom. I needed this validation from him. I've always needed verbal reassurance that I am doing a good job, whether it was as a soccer player, or a student, or a wife and mom. Words of affirmation are crucial to me. They are not to Nick, so it means a lot when he takes the time to use such words with me.

I've always taken a lot of pride in being a good mom. I can admit now—a difficult thing for me to do—that I haven't always been a perfect mom. I've let other things get in the way of being the best mom I could be over the years. One of the biggest obstacles to that goal was alcohol. My need to be perfect and to people please became a heavy load at times. So, I'd turn to alcohol to numb the feelings. I was drowning under the weight of my own expectations and the easy solution to get rid of this burden was drinking. I am thankful that I never reached rock bottom. No DUIs, no arrests, no issues with custody of my kids or losing a job. Had any of these situations affected me, it could have been a different story for me. Just one misfortune could have altered the course of my life. I'm grateful that I was spared devastating outcomes and being able to achieve forever sobriety now.

One of the first quit-lit books I read was *Quit Like a Woman*, by Holly Whitaker. I read it for the first time back in 2021. A lot of Holly's arguments about why AA wasn't a fit for her rang true for me back then and still do. The premise of her book is that opting not to drink is a radical choice in a culture that is obsessed with alcohol, and I couldn't agree more. I actually experienced this when on a trip recently with my mom, my daughter, and my sister. My sister asked if it would upset me if she ordered a drink at dinner. I felt like I needed to explain to her why I am choosing not to drink. Which is absolutely ridiculous! I do understand that my sister's question was innocent, in that it was meant to be respectful of me. But my own newly espoused convictions about drinking offer a perspective that I appreciate may be difficult to grasp. Why do we need to explain why we are choosing not to ingest poison? Why is alcohol the only addictive substance for which justification appears needed when we abstain from it? Whitaker writes, "Women and other historically marginalized and oppressed individuals are now absolutely ascendant in our power. My question is why, in the midst of this ascension and after all we have fought for, are we collectively and willingly taking ourselves down with alcohol?"[8] Great question, Holly. She answers it later in the book by explaining why women, and others who are part of a historically marginalized group, may not identify with Alcoholics Anonymous recovery

---

8   Holly Whitaker. *Quit Like a Woman: The Radical Choice to Not Drink in a Culture Obsessed with Alcohol*, The Dial Press, 2019, 39.

methods. Whitaker writes, "Often we turn to substances because we feel powerless, because existing in a world that we were told from birth is not ours to exist in the way we need to feels terrifying and limiting and defeating. Which is to say that adopting an idea of powerlessness runs the very real risk of retraumatizing us, since that was what made us sick in the first place."[9]

Indeed.

---

9   Ibid, 149.

Chapter 15

Introducing Naughty Baby
& The Shit Show of 2020

When Micah was about six months old, I started to feel those familiar feelings of early pregnancy. I had breastfed Micah off and on for the first few months. I hadn't gotten my period back, so I figured the chances of my getting pregnant were slim to none. I was wrong. When Micah was five months old, I got pregnant with Jaxon Dean. They are fourteen months apart, and Jaxon was the best surprise I didn't know I needed. Micah and Jaxon don't really know a life without each other, being so close in age. Jaxon was born on March 30, 2015. He had not wanted to wait until his scheduled C-section at four, that afternoon. My water broke in the very early morning hours of March 30. He was born via C-section around six, that morning. Jaxon was my biggest baby, weighing in at nine pounds fifteen ounces. His were the chunkiest little baby cheeks you've ever seen! My recovery from this C-section was a walk in the park compared to how things unfolded after Micah's birth. I was suddenly a mom of four. We had celebrated Micah's first birthday just a couple of months before Jaxon arrived. In that full house, my heart was full too. I suffered less anxiety after Jaxon. He was exclusively breastfed from the start, and that didn't stop until he was about two and a half years old. Our bond was different from the one I shared with the twins and Micah. It was clear to everyone for those first couple of years that I was his favorite person. Because he was to be the last baby I would have, I soaked up all of those firsts with him. I prioritized being a mom over everything else in my life, including friendships that I wish I had treated with more care at the time.

Jaxon had some medical issues around his first birthday. Because of that, I felt I had to step back and choose not to be a part of Sarah's wedding. I now look back on that decision with sadness. I don't regret it, because being there for Jaxon and not taking time away from what he needed, seemed imperative. I can see now that I might have been able to balance things better than I did. One of the greatest growing pains I've experienced in my thirties and forties is maintaining healthy friendships as an adult and as a mom, and now as a sober person—I'm still working through maintaining this balance. I missed moments with dear friends during that time of my life. But I can say that I was there every step of the way for my kids.

Being a mom of four kept me grounded, and not drinking excessively—for a while. I was working from home as a human resources consultant part-time, while raising the children. Nick worked extra shifts. We had a good life, and things were mostly steady for a few years. The boys started preschool in 2018, and I had a little more time to myself. By that point, I was in a new job as a human resources manager for a virtual staffing company. I really enjoyed the camaraderie with my coworkers. I was doing well emotionally and things in my life were balanced over all. After I stopped breastfeeding Jaxon, I still had days where I drank too much, and felt like crap the next day but I was mostly moderating. Then, March 2020 came along.

Pandemic parenting was one of the most trying situations of my adulthood thus far. Suddenly, in addition to working full-time from home, I was handling all my children at home since schools were closed and teaching was done virtually. I was now a full-time homeschool mom of a preschooler, a kindergartener, and two middle schoolers. For my younger two kids, virtual teaching meant that they had a twenty-minute Zoom meeting with their teacher once or twice a day. Then, they were expected to complete assignments online. For a five-year-old and a six-year-old, this was a near-impossible task to accomplish without the constant supervision of a parent. Because I worked remotely this responsibility fell on my shoulders most days of the week. When Nick was home from his job, he would help. Nonetheless, Micah and Jaxon were struggling in different ways with this virtual learning environment. The twins were able to manage their classes generally well, considering the virtual nature of classes and the absence of direct face-to-face instruction from March to June of 2020. At that time, no one knew how long schools were going to keep functioning virtually. The next school year, the twins were on video calls and doing school work throughout the day. They managed to keep honor roll grades despite the pandemic. Micah was doing OK. Jaxon was starting kindergarten, but on Zoom, and he struggled with that. We decided to get the two younger boys into a charter homeschool program. This strategy would give me a lot more control. I could plan out the boys' schedules and decide when assignments would be completed, when I would review lessons with them, and how we would structure our day. We were no longer at the mercy of the public school teachers' schedules for class meetings and assignment completion. I would therefore not have to move my work calls around to accommodate the classroom Zoom calls.

Jaxon's struggles did not affect him academically. He was far ahead many of his peers because of the year and a half that he spent in full-time preschool. But I distinctly remember Jaxon hiding under the kitchen table when it was time to join his kindergarten class via Zoom. I also vividly recall him spitting at the screen when another kid would answer a question before him. Such behaviors led to nick-naming Jaxon "Naughty Baby." He is still called that, lovingly, by me and his siblings and cousins. Since he's no longer a baby, sometimes he's simply "Naughty." I remember having to chase him around the house to get him to sit down for his Zoom calls. It was a nightmare. Micah, on his end, was tired of online apps for math and science. We were all going stir crazy with nothing to do. All sports activities were canceled and church was closed for a while. The absence of social outlets was overwhelming. And I was cracking under the pressure.

I started drinking again—letting alcohol creep back slowly into my life in 2020. Social media trumpeted messages like "How could moms possibly survive the pandemic without alcohol?" Our neighborhood started engaging in booze basket surprises. You could pick a name off a list of participating neighbors and deliver a basket of snacks and booze to the mom in the house. The aim was to show each other kindness. But I wondered why it had to involve alcohol. What our society tells us is drinking = survival, if you are a mom. And during the pandemic the message was only amplified.

By the end of 2021, I was miserable in my job, fighting with Nick regularly, wanting more for myself but not sure exactly what that meant, and drinking every night again. I enrolled in a teaching credential program, and was preparing to start my student teaching in the fall of 2022, when I just fell apart. I had been employed for over five years at a company. In August, I got an offer for a job at a different business. When I gave notice to my current employer, my boss offered me a promotion and a raise to stay put. I accepted his counter-offer. But I was left with the impression that I had been purchased for a higher price. So, I quickly felt trapped in that position. My happiness was a casualty of my decision to stay in that company. I stopped the teaching credential program. I no longer had the drive to pursue a different career path after accepting the counter-offer at my current job. More often than not, I would drink after work and then wake up with a hangover. I had turned forty that June. I was also experiencing more anxiety than I had in the past. One day, I felt so wretched that I convinced myself I was having a heart attack. I had called my doctor and she ordered an all-day heart monitor to be worn. I had a high heart rate, off and on throughout the day, likely caused by spikes in anxiety, but nothing of concern. A year later, I found out that plenty in my diet was not helping. I had been consuming a lot of foods high in sugar, carbohydrates in particular. I was also not exercising. These two factors contributed to the spiking heart rates. I was in the worst health of my life in 2022. I was close to three hundred pounds at my heaviest during this time. I was despondent and had sunk into self-loathing. I completed a year of online health classes through my medical insurance to qualify for gastric bypass surgery, which took place in April 2023.

Whether I was ready to admit it or not, I had an entirely unhealthy relationship with alcohol. I always came up with an excuse for why I needed to drink. In fact, the surgery had been scheduled in late 2022. But, because my blood test results in August and September of 2022 showed I was drinking alcohol, it was postponed. This delay is just one of the many times when I let alcohol get in the way of my path to be a better me.

I was approved again for gastric bypass surgery for early 2023. Around that time, Nick's parents both passed away within eleven days of each other. The emotional toll was heavy. I had gone through stints of not drinking for a week or two at a time, enough for my blood test results to come back clean. Then, as I was preparing to go out on medical leave in a couple of months, I found out the job I had held for six years was about to change drastically. The CEO of the company had sold it to an investor. I could tell from my first meeting with that investor that things would not work out there for long.

After surgery, on the day I returned from medical leave, I quit my job on the spot. The decision I made to quit might seem impulsive. It was a scary time financially letting go of a source of income without another one lined up. But I do not regret it. I felt that I had to make that choice if I had any hope of surviving the next chapter of my life. Coming out of the shit show of 2020 and 2021, I had decided to undergo this major surgery to change my life. I knew I couldn't make long-term positive changes if I stayed stagnant in my career. In addition, the impression I had had from the incoming boss had been extremely negative. I landed a new job about a month later. Still able to work remotely, I also had the opportunity to try my hand at marketing, while doing human resources work. I found out that marketing isn't for me. But the learning experience was beneficial and the position was a good transition between the spot I left and the one I'd end up in less than a year later.

I wrote a blog the day I quit that job I'd held for six years. While raw, it accurately captures how I felt about my decision that day and why I chose to do things the way I did. In particular, I did not give notice, which is out of character for me. It also goes against all my years working in human resources, silently judging those people who quit without giving any notice. This initially appeared in my blog (https://authenticallymejourney.blogspot.com). Note that what follows is reproduced as it was in the original.

Today was my first day back at work. It was also my last day at that company. I had been there for over six years and absolutely adore so many of my coworkers. But enough is enough, and when my character is called into question, when there is absolutely no regard for the human aspect of an employee, or consideration for the hard work that was put into the transition of the company, and the new owner/CEO repeats over and over that "everyone is replaceable," there's something wrong. I knew it in my gut back in March and tried to stick it out for months. I was really hoping I'd go back today after my medical leave and there'd be positivity and instead I was met with several emails discounting the work I've done as HR Director, pointing out mistakes from teammates (that weren't their mistakes—just a side effect of the transition and setting up new systems such as payroll) and accusing me of "stealing" or taking time from the company by not putting in for PTO [paid time off] on a day where I was still checking emails and had already worked over my salaried hours for that week. The thing I loved most about the company up until two months ago was the recognition that PEOPLE are your biggest asset. Not the bottom-line dollar, because that won't be there if you mistreat people. . . . There's no room for egos if you want your employees to respect you and vice versa. It's sad, but it was time for that door to close.

I cannot wait to see where I am in five years. Whether I am in a new career or not, I know that I will be healthier than ever and setting a positive example for my kids by honoring my boundaries and respecting my own curiosity and determination to be the best version of me.

Chapter 16

Grief is Love Not Wanting to Let Go

In February 2023, the loss of both of his parents within eleven days of each other shook Nick to the core. They both suffered from different forms of Parkinson's, but they had been divorced for over thirty years. My mother-in-law seemed to be waiting to let go until she knew her ex-husband had passed on. I still believe that she died of a broken heart. I think he was the one true love of her life. Although their lives didn't intersect much in the previous thirty years, she never really let him go. He was "her person," whether their marriage was still intact in the eyes of the law or not. This loss felt surreal and heartbreaking. I watched my husband suffer the most intense emotional pain I've seen him in since we met. I also saw how the death of his paternal grandparents affected my little HSP, Micah. That felt devastating.

Since I was about thirteen years old, I have battled with some form of mental health struggles. Because of the stigma of the late twentieth century regarding mental health, I believe that I had undiagnosed depression and anxiety for most of my teenage years and into adulthood. I have wondered if I have some level of bipolar disorder. However, the fact that I can usually manage symptoms unless under extreme stress seems to point to a major depressive disorder and/or anxiety disorder.

The hardest thing.

The impossible thing.

The gut-wrenching thing.

Here goes.

It's that I quite possibly gave this invisible disease to my kid, Micah. I have seen therapists over the years to address my depression and anxiety, and part of the treatment to address my mental health struggles is learning emotional regulation. The process teaches me to manage the anxiety and depression in a positive way. Its goal is to allow me not to end up crying in the closet or staying in bed for days, because the sadness just takes over my whole body. Seeing professionals about my own struggles allowed me to identify some of the same struggles in Micah. Uncovering this reality was difficult, because I carry the weight of having passed this affliction on to him. A small but insufficient comfort is the knowledge that I gained regarding my own struggles has allowed me to support Micah in his own journey.

Micah has struggled with his emotions and experienced outbursts since he was about three years old. It is when he was that age that we realized he was unable to express his discomfort with people he didn't know extremely well coming into his personal space. He clearly had difficulty dealing with people trying to hug him without permission. He also generally experienced distress when people were insistent about knowing what was going on in his head. Most of us do not enjoy being antagonized or teased, and that goes for Micah too. But, while most people might shrug off such annoyances, Micah acts out when someone pushes his buttons. He has outbursts and shows physical aggression toward his siblings. He even hit a friend of mine once, when he was a toddler, because she was teasing and poking him. Micah can be an extremely loving child. He loves his mom and dad, his grandparents, and his siblings and his cousins. I think I am the only human on this planet that he willingly comes up to and asks for a hug. He will let his dad, grandparents, siblings, cousins hug him, but he doesn't ask anyone else for a hug except for me. It feels like a privilege to be loved by Micah. It's an honor that he chooses me to be "his person." It's also the most exhausting thing in the world. It drains me of the normal mom emotions around ensuring my child's needs are met and emptying my cup to fill up his. But I struggle with the same mental health issues that he does. So, the challenge is filling his cup from a cup that's empty. I recently shared with Nick that it feels like I ran a marathon and then I have to run another one right away, but this time I'm exhausted, in physical pain, starving, and dying of thirst.

In early 2023, Micah's grandmother's funeral mass and interment service took place on a Friday. On Saturday, Micah spent most of the day with my parents, while Nick and I went to start cleaning up at Nick's mom's house. On Sunday, Micah spent most of the day with Nick and Jaxon, going to the movies, running errands, just having a nice day off together. Then, evening came, with time to settle down and get back into the routine of the week. I asked Micah to eat dinner and get in the shower. He refused. We went back and forth. I remained relatively calm, giving him time and options to make the right choice. I had to stand my ground. He's getting too old, and too big and strong for me to let him get out of control or get physical with me. In the past, he has tried to hit or kick his dad and me, when he's frustrated and feeling overwhelmed. At times, when Micah tried to hit me, all I could do to control his flailing limbs was just hold him in a tight hug, which eventually calmed him down. That Sunday evening, he threw a few things around the room and beat up on his brother's gaming chair and some furniture. After that tantrum, I told him he just needed to stay in one spot on the bed or get in the shower. He chose to stay on the bed. I told him I had to vacuum the living room rug and I'd be back in a few minutes.

While I was vacuuming, I heard him start to yell, "I'm going to hurt someone!" a few times. I waited for a few minutes, to give him time to calm down on his own before I intervened. I then went back into the room. I told him that it was a serious and frightening thing to yell. I said that there were two options. Either he needed to tell me if he was just making these threats to get my attention, because he didn't know what to do with his feelings. Or he must tell me if he meant that, in which case we would take him to the hospital to talk to a doctor who can help him. He didn't say anything. He just stared at me and started picking at his fingernails. Over the years, it had become clear that this habit developed as a reaction to the inner anxiety he feels. I told Micah that I would be back in one minute to hear what he decided, after I had finished vacuuming.

When I came back as promised, I found Micah crying. I laid down with him on the bed. He started sobbing uncontrollably, his body rocking back and forth. I ached watching his pain and hated every second that he had to endure it. I find that it is the hardest thing in the world to see my child experience the worst anguish, one that I know all too well. Hearing my child tell me that he can't breathe, he can't catch his breath, that it hurts to breathe, seeing his eyes just drowning in pain and hurt, it all breaks my heart into a million pieces, over and over again.

The loss of two parents within days of each other has to cause a pain I cannot even begin to imagine. Trying to be what Nick needed me to be during that time was beyond difficult. I felt deeply for him as he faced this loss, carried the weight of coordinating the services and the rest of the rituals, and delivered eulogies for both of his parents. But my biggest emotional challenge came from seeing Micah fall apart, knowing that in some way I had done that to him. I was haunted by the thought that I had passed down to him broken pieces of myself. I wish I could take that away. But I can't.

So for now, I'll do what I can to lighten up the emotional burden for Micah. I'll take the pain that I can carry from him and do my best to manage it for him. I'll hold him while his little body rocks back and forth. I'll talk him through what he's willing to share. I'll make sure he has people in his corner at school and at home, who know where his struggles lie. The members of this support community will be shown how to recognize the signs and help him through the harder days when I can't be right by his side.

There is plenty in my day that can be a challenge—a job that doesn't bring much joy, friendships that aren't always what I want them to be, or bumps in the road of marriage or in other close relationships, or financial struggles, or whatever other curveballs life will inevitably throw my way. But no matter how hard other things are in my day, God chose me to be Micah's mom. He chose me to be the mom to all four of my kids. For better or for worse, they're stuck with me. I sometimes feel like they got dealt the short end of the stick because of my struggles. It may be that God chose me because He knew my struggles would in some way be the lifeline that my kids needed. Perhaps I'm exactly the right mom for Micah. I know the feeling of one's body shaking uncontrollably, of one's emotions being out of control and not being able to explain why or how it got that way. Maybe the very worst thing I think I could offer my offsprings is exactly the thing that makes me the perfect person for this mom thing after all. Maybe it is in our brokenness and fragility that we find the strength to overcome the struggles we face the second or third time around.

Chapter 17

My Wake-Up Call

My daughter, Rylee, is wise beyond her years, and she is also as young as her seventeen years of age. What I mean by that is she lost her wallet recently—something unsurprising for the teenager she is, and something I know I did at that age. Academically driven and smart, Rylee can also, of course, get preoccupied by the constant distractions that pop up in a seventeen-year-old's world. But, she's also mature in quiet ways, in ways that don't demand attention, but that I notice and appreciate. She's kind, she's smart, she works hard, and she's thoughtful. She is also possibly the biggest reason why I chose forever sobriety on September 14, 2023. We were driving home from somewhere. She declared that she doesn't want to be around me when I drink. She doesn't like how I act and that I can be mean. She announced that she'll just go to her grandparents' house if I'm going to be drinking at home, because it makes her nervous and uncomfortable.

Holy shit.

That declaration was the biggest wake-up call I ever could have needed. I already knew my drinking caused problems around me. I was aware of all of this, notably because Rylee's comments were reminiscent of admonitions from Nick, in difficult prior conversations with me. I didn't drink for months after my gastric bypass because I didn't know what I could tolerate post-surgery. But, gradually, like always, I started drinking one or two here and there. By early September 2023, it had become the same old pattern. I had my last drinks on September 13, 2023, which happens to be my mom's birthday. My mom and my sister were in Orange County visiting my nieces. That night, I just went into yet another drinking binge. I woke up on September 14th knowing that I would never drink again.

Chapter 18

My Reliance on Alcohol & My Resilience in Life

It's been sixty days, guys! Sixty days sober. Sixty days of doing the work to figure out why I drank, what it was masking, and how to make positive changes for the long haul. A mindset shift occurred over the course of the last two months. I'm no longer thinking, "Wouldn't it be nice to stop at CVS after school pickups and just numb out for a couple of hours with a bottle of vodka or whiskey?" Now, if that thought even creeps anywhere near my consciousness, I remember how much I love my sober sleep, and it's gone in a flash. I've always loved my sleep. I just never realized how much alcohol was screwing with my REM cycle. Now that I've done the work of researching and learning from experts in the sober community, I know there is no going back for me.

When you have an unhealthy relationship with alcohol, you endure four in the morning wake-ups, sometimes sweating, sometimes nauseous, and always with heart and mind racing out of control. In addition to the disrupted sleep, alcohol wreaks havoc on your body, specifically your brain, your heart, your liver, and your immune system. As Annie Grace details in her trailblazing book, *This Naked Mind*, "Alcohol slows the pace of communication between neurotransmitters. It interrupts your brain's communication pathways, literally reducing the speed of communication between parts of your brain by slowing down your brain's neural highways."[10] Alcohol specifically gets in the way of the major functions of your body. Your carefully constructed body, alcohol breaks down piece by piece. Why do we willingly sign up for the disrupted sleep, the breakdown in brain communication, and the racing heart (among other things)? Because we have been conditioned to believe that alcohol will make us feel better, not worse. Because we live in a society where the pressures to succeed and be the best are overwhelming on a good day and impossible on the bad ones. Because we are drowning in expectations and unable to cope with the day-to-day demands placed on us. There are so many reasons why we choose to drink. But there are so many more reasons why I chose to stop.

Sixty days of sobriety has brought me a lot of clarity on things I don't miss from my drinking days. The "hangxiety" (a combination of a hangover and anxiety) for one—that feeling, the next day, that you've completely screwed everything up, you'd do anything for a nap, and your heart is racing uncontrollably. I remember back in the fall of 2022: I went through a full day of heart monitoring because I was convinced I kept having a heart attack. I was in a constant cycle of drinking almost every night. Then, I would wake up feeling exhausted because I never hit that REM sleep cycle. But I was also filling up on carbs because I couldn't stomach anything else in my constant state of sleep deprivation and hangovers.

Sobriety has brought me a lot of clarity about the ways I failed to appreciate people in my life, who suffered through the ups and downs right along with me. I thought I found my forever love when I was sixteen, but I was wrong. I didn't actually meet my forever love until I was twenty-seven years old. He was everything I knew I

---

10   Annie Grace. *This Naked Mind: Control Alcohol, Find Freedom, Discover Happiness & Change Your Life*, Penguin Random House, 2018, 63.

needed. I wasn't emotionally ready for the kind of relationship that he could share with me, because I was broken from past relationships. I had been married before and should have been ready for the kind of forever love that he showed to me. But I was too damaged at the time to really appreciate it or him. Something deep inside me knew that I needed it and him, though I couldn't fully accept or embrace it. What follows is my public apology to the man I never knew I needed, but without whom I know now I wouldn't have such a beautiful life. It initially appeared in my blog (https://authentical-lymejourney.blogspot.com/). Note that what follows is reproduced as it was in the original.

Nick, you have always been my rock. You've been the calm in the often stormy, chaotic, emotional roller coaster that I've brought you on over the last 14 years. I know I have not treated you like I should for the last (almost) 13 years we've been married, and I want you to know (and everyone else who reads my blog... all 5 of you kind souls out there) that I am so sorry for that. I have made mistakes and treated you unkindly, and not shown you the type of forever love that you've shown me and that you always deserved from me. Yet, I'm beyond grateful that I knew somewhere in the pit of my soul that I needed you. Everything about you was and is the perfect balance to me. You're the calm, I'm the storm. You're the rock-solid foundation to hold things up when my crazy ass gets emotional and impulsive and wants to save the world or shake things up or whatever torrent of emotion and passion is coursing through me at the time. You are the rational and pragmatic to my emotional and passionate decision-making. But you are also sarcastic and funny (sometimes, but I'm funnier, don't forget that) and loving in your own way. You have shown me in so many ways over the past 14 years that you said "I do" and "forever" and meant every word. There was never another option for you. I'm sorry if I ever made you feel like there was another door for me to go through, another option other than this forever with you.

Thank you for loving me through my brokenness over the years. Thank you for supporting me even when supporting me meant saying things I thought were "mean" or "harsh." I know with every fiber of my being that you are not a mean-spirited person, and anything you've said to me about my choices along the way were meant with good intentions and true concern for my well-being, whether that was physical, mental, or emotional. You've seen the weight of other people's stuff that I carry, and you've asked to help lighten the load. Whether or not I let you help was my fault, I should have trusted that anything I gave to you to help me would be cared for with the same concern and thought that you put into any decision you make, as painstakingly drawn out as I feel your process can be at times. You slow me down. You calm me. As we go through this lovely process of home renovations, I've told you that sleeping next to you makes me breathe easier. My anxiety slows down, my heart is happy, and I feel safe. That's what you've always been to me, and more. You make me laugh, you make my heart race (in a good way), and you hold me like you don't want to let go. Even when I have pushed you away or not prioritized you like I should have, you have always been there ready to accept me back with open arms.

Your support of my sobriety, my pursuit of other career goals and ambitions, and my journey to get healthy and recover from my RNY [gastric bypass] surgery this year have been so reassuring and steady. You make me a better person just by accepting me for all of my flaws and brokenness and cheering me on when I work to put back the pieces and do better.

I am grateful for this forever love. It may sometimes look boring and passive and quiet from the outside, but from my perspective, it's exactly what I need and have always wanted, even if I didn't know it in 2009. I knew there was something about you and our love that needed to be in my life, and I'm so glad that we are where we are today. You are my favorite person.

Jenn Burton

Chapter 19

Scars & Healing

When I was growing up, being an empath wasn't a thing. People were emotional or they weren't, and that was that. Now, being an empath is something that a lot of people identify with, and the more I learn about myself, the more I am convinced that I am an empath. My weakness can be that I care too much about things and people and situations. So, then, I get too deep in trying to fix it and end up causing more damage. That has happened to me in friendships over the years. Thus, I have to catch myself these days from trying to fix everything for my kids, especially my teenagers, because I'm not doing them any favors by always being on cleanup crew. They need to learn how to fix things. Even more importantly, they have to figure out how to sit in the ugly and not fixable for a minute, because that's a critical life skill and a crucial part of growing up.

Scars have been a part of my journey. When my ex-husband and I first broke up right after high school for a month or so, I covered a scar resulting from self-harm with a tattoo that says, "Let's compare scars" and I think that's a quiet thing that we all do—compare scars. We talk about our trauma and we share our war stories, comparing whose is worse. What I've come to realize in the last several months is that my scar may feel to me like it weighs as heavily on me as

115

another person's scars weighs on him or herself. We all bleed, we are all in pain, we are all going through something. The important thing is to figure out how to make it hurt a little less, how to be the best versions of ourselves, and to keep pushing forward.

Things got extremely difficult for me in March of 2023. I was going through a tough time personally. I was struggling with big changes at my job. I was struggling with making the decision to get bariatric surgery. And I was struggling with my mental health—not being on the right dose of medication for depression and anxiety. For a really tough few weeks, I was crying constantly and unable to control my emotions. On one of those bad days, I cut myself, which led to scars on my thigh that have made me very self-conscious since. For my birthday that year, I decided to turn these scars into something beautiful. I wanted it to match the existing owl tattoo, which was already on my thigh, just to the side of the fresh scars. So, I settled on a dreamcatcher design, and found a local artist who could make it her own. I am so happy with how it came out, and even more at peace with not seeing the constant reminder of my pain etched on my skin. A lovely artistic creation transformed the symbol of an ugly and painful experience.

People ask me why I have certain tattoos, what their meanings are, and if I regret any of them. I only regret the giant roses on my chest—they are huge and hard to cover on work Zoom calls. I am in the process of getting them laser removed. Every other piece of artwork on my body I can trace back to a certain time in my life. The tattoo design itself may not have meaning behind it, but the moment in time when I got that tattoo is significant in my journey. My tattoos represent a collage of moments in my life and they matter to me because they all contribute to how I constructed my life, warts and all.

I'm grateful to live in a time when I am able to use art to share what matters in my life on my own body. I feel fortunate to exist in an age when tattoo artists don't judge self-harm nor shame those who are afflicted by this disorder. I'm not proud to have inflicted such injuries to my own body, but these events are part of my life experiences all the same. The tattoos are a reminder that each time I stumbled and fell back into old habits, I hoped and prayed that I wouldn't falter in the future, but I could never be certain. All I could do was keep putting one foot in front of the other and move forward. This dreamcatcher tattoo means holding onto my dreams, chasing the ones that I choose, and appreciating all of the moments that got me here, including the darkest of them all.

I'm also very thankful for my online sober community of women that have become my very best friends. Sharing my journey with others who are traveling a similar road, and connecting on a more profoundly honest level than I've ever allowed myself to do: it has all been powerfully healing. I'd kept these walls up, these boundaries, because I didn't want anyone to see my vulnerabilities. I've let in these women, my Ellies, a small group from Lighthouse Sobriety. And they've let me in.

I've also been able to heal through my writing. Blogging a couple of times a week has allowed me to reignite the creative spark that had been left dormant for so long. I had lost myself in motherly duties and the daily grind. So, I had to let fall to the side those things that allowed me to take care of myself at one point in my life. I'm able to permit myself to return to these activities slowly but surely. I am thus making my way back toward the me I know I'm supposed to be. Scars and all.

Chapter 20

Eighty Days

I haven't had a drink in eighty days. I've lost more than eighty pounds in the last seven months, since my gastric bypass surgery. My mind is clearer than it's ever been. I've learned much about myself, as I make my way through book after book of sober memoirs, and self-help and transformational stories. My journey may not have been easy, but it's mine.

I don't know that I'd ever truly felt that real power—the conviction that something is wholly mine—up until this point. I found my power in my roles—as wife, daughter, mom, sister, or friend. I hadn't found my true power deep within my own self. I find a lot of the messages in the quit lit and sober culture I've immersed myself in over the past few months to be empowering, which I really appreciate. Whenever I've struggled with self-injury, or self-worth, or self-sabotage, in the past, I've felt weak and controlled by those behaviors or choices. On this new journey, I feel empowered to make positive changes for myself. I am emboldened not to let anyone or anything else control the direction in which I'm headed. In the past, I forced myself to be someone else, in order to fit in, to be accepted, to be loved and wanted. The more I discover who I am and what makes me happy, the more fitting in and being accepted by others just do not matter as much or at all. My struggles with my weight and my self-worth attached to those issues led me to feel disconnected from my own body. But now, I am starting to feel comfortable in my own skin again.

Being a people pleaser has been one of the biggest obstacles I have had to confront in the last forty-two years. This compulsion has been a burden and a challenge. Letting go of it has been extremely therapeutic for me. To release the obligation to take care of everyone else's emotions all the time has been freeing—it is not my responsibility, nor my weight to carry. I'm holding myself accountable for sitting in my own feelings, for processing the choices I've made, the mistakes, and taking ownership of the pain I may have caused others. By doing that, I'm releasing myself of the duty to hold myself accountable to everyone else, to keep them happy at all times.

Even as a mom, my responsibility is in a lot of ways to teach my kids how to be accountable for themselves and to themselves. I can't carry the load of each of their stresses. But I can help them through the process of taking on the management of their struggles for themselves. I can show them how to cope with their stress, how to be responsible for their words and actions, and how to ignore the noise of other people's opinions, social media standards of perfection, and the comparison trap with their peers. One of the most difficult and rewarding aspects of my parenting journey thus far has beeAn1 learning how to guide my kids through various paths, but also   aletting them choose which path to follow. I am teaching them how to manage expectations put on them by society, or teachers, or coaches, or friends. For instance, on a day he has to attend volleyball practice, work an evening shift at his part-time job, and prepare for a test, Lucas learns to manage his time to complete all of the tasks, or leave volleyball practice early to study before his work shift begins. I show my children that, faced with competing expectations, they need to learn how to manage their time, prioritize tasks and obligations, and respect their own limitations. I impart to them the importance of learning how to keep adapting to a constantly evolving world, how to make decisions for themselves—something I never learned. Not knowing better, I endeavored to make decisions that I thought other people wanted me to make, to try to keep people around me happy, and damaging myself in the process. I want to teach my kids that there are healthy and constructive ways to manage struggles and take accountability for our own choices.

Chapter 21

Not Everyone Grows with Us

If I were to identify a few of my most significant friendships over the years, there's a handful that come to mind. My sister was obviously my first best friend—most of us with older siblings can probably relate to that. Siblings are the friends that we never knew we needed, right? My bestie in kindergarten was Natalie, whom I have already introduced you to. Our friendship is one that doesn't need constant attention or nurturing. Whenever one needs the other, we both know we have each other's back. Our friendship is built on admiration and a lifetime of love. In late elementary school and middle school, Danielle*, Sarah, and Kenzie were my closest friends. They are all women I am still in contact with today. With some of them, it is a long-distance relationship, but these friendships, which sustained us through the teenage years upheavals, remain cherished. In addition to Laura, I met in high school two other girlfriends, and one of them I am still very close to today. I am lucky to have met amazing and strong women in high school and to still carry love for them today.

Most of my friendships do not require frequent get-togethers or phone calls. But these friends all know that I will always be there for them. I know that our bond will stand the test of time, even if we

---

* Some names in this story have been changed for privacy reasons.

rarely see each other face to face. My first husband and I had a group of friends, and some of the women among them are people I adore to this day. Over time, the connections with others ended. I still mourn their loss, because they were very significant through some of the toughest times of my life. But I understand and accept that our life journeys have taken a different route. Callie was one of these friends with whom I didn't see eye to eye, as we went into different stages of our lives. I had four kids and a focus on settling into my life. She pursued living her best life and continuing to have fun.

I'm grateful for the times that I and these once deeply loved friends had together and the memories we forged. I wish they go on experiencing the very best in their lives. I have also made new mom friends over the last ten years, since we moved to our current neighborhood. A few of them hold a very special place in my heart, because the ups and downs we've faced together in motherhood solidified our bond. Some have moved away, and I am no longer in contact with them. But I always will hold love and respect for them too.

And then there is the friendship that has been a soft place to land for close to two decades. It has also been a very emotionally charged friendship, almost since the beginning. This is one of those friendships that you know was meant to be a part of your life—beause the connection is so strong and so immediate. But, sometimes, the path that we have each been on and what we have held dear and wanted to protect and preserve have no longer aligned with one another. This friendship has faced a lot of highs and lows. We've stopped communicating, at times for months and even years, possibly because one of us might have misspoken and offended the other. Or the vagaries of life might have intervened and we were each going through them in our own way. We live in different states, so we've spent long weekends or weeks together on vacation. We met through a mutual friend and instantly clicked. Thus, over the years, Heather has been a friend that I can share anything with. I can't imagine not having her in my life. I know that she feels the same way about me.

I am sad about some situations surrounding my friendship with Heather. For example, I regret not being there for her as much as I should have, when her mom passed away suddenly, the month when I married Nick. She has shut me out for various reasons over the years, and I've shut her out of my life on occasion too. I've missed out on important events in her life, and she's missed out on significant moments in mine. I know I will always have love for her.

In reflecting at length on my life, my choices, and my hopes for the future, the relationship I have had with Heather has come into focus. Thus, as I reassess and reevaluate my values and preferences, at each stage, this friendship appears more and more unfit to my newly developing standards. My sobriety journey has opened my eyes to what is healthy for me and what is not. My priorities have become clearer. What now takes precedence includes protecting my peace and sobriety, and my husband and my kids. Spending quality time with my grandmother, my parents, my siblings and my nieces and nephews comes next in line. Refocusing on my career and taking care of myself are also at the top of my priority list these days. Self-care for me involves getting a lot of sleep, reading quit lit, walking and moving my body every day, eating well, and getting my nails done regularly. Creating solid relationships with people who share similar priorities, including sobriety, is also important.

I've learned that sometimes we have to let go of friendships in order to be the most authentic version of ourselves. At times, we have to grieve the loss of a friendship. We need to stop chasing the expectations from someone else and what they want us to be. Taking such steps hurts. In my case, it also comes with the certainty that this is the healthiest choice for me and my sobriety. I used to think that drinking was my coping mechanism to deal with the stress of parenting. I thought confronting stress was about surviving. But I failed to see that simply appreciating the mundane aspects, every day, in parenting, marriage, and life would free me from the weight of anxiety. I turned to friends and others, who would tell me that what I was doing was OK. In hindsight, in reality, I was destroying my body, my mental health, my marriage, and my relationship with my kids. In many books I have read over the last several months, in my sobriety, I have learned that some people have a problem with gray area drinking. Commonly used in sobriety circles, "gray area drinking" refers to what an individual who doesn't fit the definition of an alcoholic does. Such a person is high functioning, doesn't appear to be in danger of losing job or family, and is, at least on the surface, keeping it together. Yet, alcohol is a foundationally tricky thing for them to manage, and despite multiple attempts to moderate, they are unable to do so. I have come to find out how our body chemistry and nutrition play a role in unhealthy drinking habits. As I understand more about the science behind my unhealthy relationship with drinking, I see links with my unhealthy relationships as well. The relationships I tried to destroy because they didn't align with my bad choices (to drink, specifically) were the ones I should have been trying to save all along. The friendships that were contributing to my unhealthy life choices I should have jettisoned instead. In trying to justify my drinking choices, I was choosing all of the wrong aspects to focus on in other areas of my life.

So, the future I look toward is of being authentically me. I intend on pursuing things that uplift me and on creating positive side effects in my life rather than hangovers and feelings of guilt. Thus, I am not going to continue to chase a friendship, such as the one with Heather, that has done more to create negativity and feelings of failure for me. I'm going to honor the friendship and what it has been for me over the past twenty years. But I am not going to prioritize it over my mental health, my sobriety, my marriage, my relationship with my kids, or even my career. If the friendship redevelops at some point, as a positive addition to the new world of authenticity that I'm creating, awesome. If not, I will let it go and stop holding on to it so tightly that it can't breathe, and therefore, can't survive. I will grieve the loss of that friendship while still being grateful for the beautiful memories that it created for us. I will always think of Heather with love and gratitude, but also with an understanding that maybe sometimes we grow apart from people as we grow toward becoming our best selves.

Chapter 22

Pivots

Alcohol hasn't been a part of my life for one hundred and thirty-two days. Since beginning my sobriety journey in September 2023, I've made a few pivots. I have determined that I am not in a place where I want to start a career from scratch. So, in January 2024, I re-evaluated my career in human resources, and committed to finding a job within a field that aligns with where I'm headed personally. I landed a job with an organization that focuses on culture, accountability, and implementing change from the inside out for businesses across the globe. I'm settling into my new role. In the process, I am reminding myself that we get out of our career what we put into it. I'm working longer days than I have in a while. However, I'm finding fulfillment in my interactions with colleagues. I am experiencing gratification in the ways that I am being challenged to step up, take accountability, and be the change that we want to see in organizations that my company works with. I seek to model the behavior that we want others to follow. By being a leader in this way and owning my part of the journey, I'm positively affecting others around me. Maybe human resources isn't the field I initially intended to work in, but it's where I am now. And for now, it allows me to grow and also to pursue the things I'm passionate about, my family, my writing, and my sobriety.

As I reflect back on the last forty-two years, some of the hard times feel as recent as yesterday. Many of the memories that come up as I write have long been forgotten in the nooks and crannies of my mind. Our brains are amazing things. They protect us from past trauma. They hide the truth when we aren't ready to face it. They bounce back when we decide it's time to flex those creative muscles once again. My reaction to stress or uncomfortable situations in the past was flight. It would urge me to get the hell out of there, to make it all less uncomfortable. Over the past several months, I have observed that I often no longer default to flight mode. If I do, I have enough confidence and the ability to wait it out to not make hasty decisions. I may be feeling that flight in my bones, but I don't act on it. For me, this is growth. Huge growth.

Within my first few weeks at the new job in 2024, I traveled to an offsite company kickoff meeting. I was very anxious about this gathering, because I hadn't interacted in person with work colleagues in over ten years. I worked remotely way before COVID. There are pros and cons with work-from-home life. The balance can be challenging. But, being able to attend all of the kids' awards, sports competitions, and spelling bees, and to volunteer on occasion, has been invaluable.

I was on information overload by the second day. Not only was I in back-to-back meetings all day, I was forced to "people" for hours on end. As an introvert, I find it difficult to deal with people for hours and hours. It drains me. And to top it off, these were all brand new people whom I had never met or with whom I had had one or two online meetings. The icing on the cake was when a few people asked me questions that I don't yet know the answer to, because I had started this job, with this company, a mere three weeks before.

It. Was. A. Lot.

So, by that second day, I was starting to question whether or not I had made the right decision to take this job. The familiar flight response was taking shape within my gut, and I immediately wanted to react and make things less uncomfortable for myself. At the root of it, I think my tank was empty. Yet, one thing kept rolling through my mind: human resources is not an area that sets my soul on fire, but I was feeling energized by these people. My new coworkers' commitment to changing the culture across organizations in different industries around the world, and the warm welcome they extended to me as a new member of their team impressed me and spoke volumes about this company. I talked to my husband about how I was feeling and came to the realization, I. Am. Exactly. Where. I. Am. Supposed. To. Be.

It has become clear to me that, right now, I don't want to start a new career. I don't want to be at the bottom of the earning scale or racking up student debt. I don't want to feel uncertainty on a daily basis again. This role is exactly what I have wanted my entire career in human resources. But my career doesn't have to be everything to me. Passion, I can find in the other things that fill my life. Options for fulfilment mean more involvement in my online sober communities, continuing to be a mentor to teenagers in my community, becoming a sober life coach, blogging, or podcasting, or writing this book. I can do all of that while having an impact through a company that truly values culture and its employees.

Before I got sober, I always had to fill up my plate, and overflow it in most cases, with things that made me feel something. Volunteering for all the kids' school activities, being team mom for every sports team they join, volunteering in the nursery at church, or taking on all the extra things that come at us in life. But these last few months have shown me that it's OK to be content where you are. There is nothing wrong with appreciating the value in the flexibility of a remote role with a good group of people, and being a positive influence on my kids and my circle of people. I may not be where I thought I would be a year ago, but I'm in a way better place in so many ways. And I'm exactly where I'm supposed to be.

Chapter 23

Sharing My Story

My breakup with alcohol one hundred and forty-six days ago has proven to be one of the single best decisions I've ever made in my life. And on February 6, 2024, I did something that scared the shit out of me. But it felt like I had removed five hundred pounds off my shoulders once it was done. On that day, I shared my sober story on Lighthouse Sobriety (LHS), the first online sober community I joined back in September. I was very anxious leading up to this moment. I had written out my story and gone over it several times. I had rehearsed and clocked myself just like I would have for an oral presentation in college! I thought I'd be reading from my script most of the time. But, once I started talking, it all came out naturally. It was an incredible experience to share my story out loud with women who have traveled a similar road. One of my favorite humans in the world, my bestie from kindergarten, Natalie, has shown up for me in crazy big and small ways since we were five years old. She showed up for me in that meeting and her presence meant more to me than I can ever convey. Her attendance of this occasion brought me to tears. She's been part of her own sober community for eighteen years. Natalie is such an inspiration and brings such a sense of comfort to me. The women I've met in LHS through my small group also all showed up for me at the meeting and with messages of love and support. I'm so grateful.

I shared in my story that day how much my life has improved since I got sober. I'll be celebrating five months of sobriety on Valentine's Day 2024. I have seen the great strides, and even growing pains, in myself mentally and emotionally. My relationship with my husband and my kids has changed meaningfully. I can now set healthy boundaries with people, friends, and work, without guilt, because I am learning that people pleasing is toxic to me. It was particularly difficult for me to share about instances when I drank and made bad choices or was mean to someone I love. I found it utterly uncomfortable to talk about my addiction to cutting and self-harm. My life has been a crazy winding path of ups and downs. Sharing the details of my struggles out loud surrounded by love, support, and acceptance was incredibly healing.

I treasure my sobriety. I'm thankful for my sober community. I'm grateful for my kids and my husband, my parents and my grandma, and my siblings and my friends. I'm grateful for a few of my favorite things looking like a cup of coffee and a book instead of a bottle of whiskey and lost memories. No matter what your struggle is in life, you can always make different choices. I'm so thankful I chose this new life, this forever sobriety on September 14, 2023. It's opened doors to a new perspective on my career, and my renewed passion for writing and reading and showing up as my authentic self.

Chapter 24

Out of the Fog

As I put the finishing touches on this book, I am celebrating nine months of choosing to walk away from alcohol as a self-medicating, numbing agent. I spent decades leaning on it, when I felt like life was getting too heavy, too messy, or too uncomfortable. In the past year, I've lost close to one hundred pounds. I've completely changed my life. I'm happier, I'm healthier. I'm purpose-driven and fulfilled by the little things that I missed when I was numbing my pain with unhealthy choices in food and alcohol. I feel better at age forty-two than I did at any age in my twenties and thirties.

Over the past nine months on this sobriety journey, I've made friends that I now consider to be some of my besties. They have walked a path that may not look exactly like mine, but that led them to the same decision that I made nine months ago. They are the truest kind of friends I have ever known because I have shown them who I truly am, with all my imperfections and my faults. And they love and accept me for who I am, despite all of my flaws. We share challenges and successes, and they are my biggest cheerleaders. These friendships have helped me get closer to realizing a cherished dream of mine: writing this book.

As a result of these sober connections, I had the pleasure of meeting one of my favorite quit lit authors, Peggi Cooney, who penned

This Side of Alcohol. I originally read her book in my first couple of months of sobriety, when I was devouring every piece of quit lit by a woman that I could find. She wrote the following, which resonates with me even more now that I've had some time to settle into my sobriety, "Sobriety has taught me the art of purposefully taking a pause, waiting a few seconds before speaking, a gift born from mindfulness."[11]

I, too, have learned this lesson, in sobriety. I've also learned that now is the time to chase the dream that I wasn't equipped to handle years ago when I was still drinking. Writing has always been a passion of mine, and now I get to see it through to a finished product that I can share with the world. It's terrifying and exhilarating all at the same time. I worry about what my family will think, what my kids will think, what my friends will think. But I am also so excited to finally be putting something like this into action.

Peggi goes on later in her book to talk about how she responded when her husband asked when she might be done with "all the meetings, courses, work" she was doing in her sobriety. Peggi's answer echoes deeply in me. In her words, "I took a big breath and calmly answered: 'No, I am not done. I will most likely never be done. It has become my life's purpose.'"[12]

I concur, Peggi.

I feel that deeply. I've worked in a field that I don't love for the last two decades. However, I do love that my job affords me the ability to prioritize my kids and their activities, while still having a career that helps me make a difference and in which I can continue to grow. I enjoy a lot of aspects of my profession. But now, my life's purpose has also started to shine through, just like sunlight breaks through the haze of the fog on a chilly winter morning. I think my purpose is to raise four productive and kind human beings. I also aspire to affect

---

11   Peggi Cooney. *This Side of Alcohol*, Leaning Rock Press, 2021, 91.
12   Ibid, 92.

the world in a way that shines a positive light on sobriety, allows me to share my thoughts in written words, and creates connections within the sober community of women that enrich my life.

Over these past nine months, I have turned a new page in my life's story. I've been reintroduced to who I am and who I was always meant to be—because somewhere along the way, I forgot about that girl. Sobriety has allowed me to truly show up as my best self every day, and to chase the dreams I had long since tossed to the wayside.

Life outside of the fog of alcohol is truly beautiful, friends. I can't wait to see what happens next.

Acknowledgements

This book wouldn't have been possible if I didn't have the support of my parents, first and foremost. I am aware that I was not the easiest child to raise, but I hope my sparkling personality and wit as an adult has made up for some of those tougher teenage years. You have both always encouraged me, supported me, and loved me, even through some of my bad decisions. Thank you for being the best parents a girl could ask for. I adore you both, and am endlessly grateful for your love.

To my husband, Nicholas: you are the calm to my storm. Thank you for loving me through all of the dark times and still wanting to hang out with me fifteen years later. Your quiet persistence and love has allowed me the space to become who I needed to be. Thank you for walking this journey of life alongside me, and doing your best to support me in all of my adventures.

To my Rylee girl. You are the best pieces of me, and I can't wait to see what you do in this life. Don't let anyone tell you that you feel too much, or love too big. Those are the qualities that are going to make you a life changer. You've already changed mine more than you realize. I love you more than all of the stars in the sky, and even better, I really like you as a human.

To my firstborn, my strong-willed, charismatic, charming, intelligent Lucas. You challenge me on the daily, and I see the best pieces of your biological dad in you. I also see the best pieces of me in you, and I'm proud of all that you've done and everything you'll accomplish in this life. Don't let the absence of some people in your life overshadow the immense presence of people who love and care about you more than words can say. I adore you, and I will love you forever.

To my wise old man trapped in a 10-year-old body, Micah Daniel. You will forever be my anchor to the things and people that keep me grounded. Your ability to feel what other people feel and sense the emotional climate in any space is incomparable. You are going to do amazing things in life, Micah. I can't wait to get a front row seat to all of your accomplishments and adventures. I love you, and I am so proud of the young man you are becoming. Don't let anyone tell you that you can't do something, because you are the most determined person I know. You can achieve anything you set your mind to, I promise.

To the best surprise I never knew I needed, my sometimes sweet and often feisty Jaxon Dean. You will always be my naughty baby, and I will forever be in the front row cheering you on in life, buddy. You are sunshine and clouds, and sugar and spice. From soccer superstar to stellar student, you are going to accomplish whatever you set your mind to, I have no doubt about that. I can't wait to see what life brings your way, and I will love you forever.

To Grandma Bev, Faith, Ashley, Sarah, Tara, Tina, Natalie, Jake and the Ellie's - you've always cheered me on, stood by my side, and rooted for me. That support and love means the world to me, and I can't thank you enough for your impact on my life. Special shout out to Koren, Kim, Melissa, and Victoria for being early readers of my manuscript. Your feedback and encouragement is so appreciated.

To my sister, I know some of this is hard to read. Never forget for a moment that I love you and we'll be bonded for life, even if that looks different than what we may have hoped for as kids.

To my amazing publisher, Robin Nelson at Leaning Rock Press, and incredible editor extraordinaire, Florence Boisse-Kilgo, thank you for your guidance throughout this process and your patience and professionalism. You are both absolute rock stars! Special thanks to Peggi Cooney for the introduction to Robin. And also a huge shoutout to Robin for the beautiful cover art.

Finally, to anyone struggling with being a highly sensitive person or an empath in a big, feelings-fueled world, it is possible to step out of the fog and live a happy life despite all of the noise around you. And to all of my fellow moms looking for that nightly escape in a wine glass or tumbler of mixed drinks, I promise no drink can compare to the feeling of being a fully present mom and having your kids want you to be there for every big and little moment. Put down the drink and go live your life to the fullest with the people who love you most in this world. Breaking up with alcohol will be the best choice you ever made, and it will give you the power to live a life full of purpose and passion.

Resources

Lighthouse Sobriety: https://joinlighthousesobriety.com

The Sober Mom Life Cafe: https://thesobermomlife.com

This Side of Alcohol: https://thissideofalcohol.com

Sobersis; Sober Minded Sisterhood: https://www.sobersis.com

REFERENCES

American Addiction Centers, "More People Are Drinking…" https://americanaddictioncenters.org/media/more-people-are-drinking-while-working-from-home-during-covid-19

Aron, Elaine. *The Highly Sensitive Person*, Kensington Publishing Corp., 1996.

Cooney, Peggi. *This Side of Alcohol*, Leaning Rock Press, 2021.

Doyle, Glennon. *Untamed*, New York:, The Dial Press, 2020.

Grace, Annie. *This Naked Mind: Control Alcohol, Find Freedom, Discover Happiness & Change Your Life, New York*, Penguin Random House, 2018.

Rzadkowolska, Karolina. *Euphoric: Ditch Alcohol and Gain a Happier, More Confident You*, HarperCollins Focus LLC, 2022.

Whitaker, Holly. *Quit Like a Woman: The Radical Choice to Not Drink in a Culture Obsessed with Alcohol*, The Dial Press, 2019.

Yvonne, Celeste. *It's Not About the Wine: The Loaded Truth behind Mommy Wine Culture*, Broadleaf Books, 2023.

About the Author

Jenn Burton is a mom of four who was born and raised in Southern California. Jenn has been married to her husband, Nick, for 14 years, and has spent the last couple of decades working in Human Resources. Her dream as a kid was to be a writer or journalist living in New York City, and she earned her Master's degree in American Studies from Cal State University, Fullerton.

Growing up a perfectionist and struggling with self-injury, depression and anxiety starting in her teen years, Jenn's journey to sobriety hasn't been easy, but it's been 100% worth it. Learning to go against the "good girl" mentality of being brought up in a culture that teaches girls to suppress their strengths and highlights their weaknesses, Jenn is now focused on pursuing a life full of authenticity, purpose and passion.

When she's not working, reading, or writing on her blog, you can find Jenn on the sidelines of her kids' various sports and school activities. She revels in being a "crazy sports mom," and enjoys occasional lunch or breakfast dates with her husband while the kids are in school.

To find out more about Jenn, visit her blog at:
https://authenticallymejourney.blogspot.com/

.